Advance praise for

WOMAN HOUSE

"Fiercely written, full of urgency and daring, *Woman House* tears at the structures and constrictions passed down from one generation to the next. Each rupture of memory is a painful exposure, the telling and untelling and retelling a balm to the mother wound. Part treatise, part confession, part interrogation, all of it tinted with anger, love, curiosity, and compassion, *Woman House* is a meditation on the desire for desire—a love song to the unsated self."

—KIM BARNES, author of *In the Wilderness: Coming of Age in Unknown Country*, Pulitzer Prize Finalist

"At once intimate, surgical, elliptical, and probing, these essays explore womanhood and daughterhood through the lens of art, pleasure, and trauma. Westerfield finds meaning in the smallest acts and rituals, trying to make sense of what it means to live authentically in and with the body. A feverish, glowing book."

—AYŞEGÜL SAVAŞ, author of *The Anthropologists*

"Lauren Westerfield's *Woman House* is a beautiful study of environment and how it is a living, breathing entity just as much as the people who move within it. Through her hauntingly elegant writing, *Woman House* walks us through the environments of the heart, of the self and body, and of the family. This all converges into a moving story of the relationships with not only ourselves but also with those we hold most closely to our hearts. Westerfield's essays notice the shifts in life both subtle and obvious and invite us into the discoveries, too. She leaves each of us a little bit changed, a bit more reflective, and a lot more connected to the world."

—ATHENA DIXON, author of *The Loneliness Files*

"This is a book about love and transformation. A memoir of loving and caring for a mother with whom she has an enduring but complex relationship, *Woman House* chronicles how a young woman learns to write her own story instead of accepting the cookie-cutter narratives this society is so quick to force the minds and bodies of women into. A beautifully written account of coming to know and accept oneself, *Woman House* is a book that invites readers to greet the world and themselves with tenderness and care."

—KATHRYN NUERNBERGER, author of *HELD: Essays in Belonging*

"This is a book interested in what happens to our self-knowledge when we understand new things about our family history, in the traumas that are passed down to us, and what sense we make of them. Along the way, Westerfield explores Louise Bourgeois's art, old Hollywood films, the writing of Beat poet Joanne Kyger, and Jane Austen's novels, as well as medical research and the language of visual arts to explore spirals, repetition, personal habits, and family patterns. Westerfield deftly twists these many threads into her own kind of spirals, then untangles, until this sharp, complex, layered read becomes a reckoning, an unfurling."

—ARIANNE ZWARTJES, author of *These Dark Skies*

"Rendered in gorgeous language, *Woman House* traces the sometimes-fraught relationship between the narrator and her mother, amplified by the pandemic. Each of these essays reveal what it means to live inside a woman's body, through illness and aging and sexual violence. A collection that is both deeply thoughtful and deeply personal, *Woman House* imagines a way forward, even when our bodies and our memories fail."

—LAURA FURLAN, author of *Indigenous Cities: Urban Indian Fiction and the Histories of Relocation*

WOMAN HOUSE

WOMAN HOUSE

ESSAYS AND
ASSEMBLAGES

LAUREN W. WESTERFIELD

UNIVERSITY OF MASSACHUSETTS PRESS
Amherst and Boston

Printed in the United States of America

This is a work of nonfiction. However, some names and identifying details of individuals have been altered to protect their privacy, and dialogue has been reconstructed from memory.

ISBN 978-1-62534-923-1 (paper)

Designed by Jen Jackowitz
Set in FreightText Pro
Printed and bound by Books International, Inc.

Cover design by adam b. bohannon
Cover art by Cristina Conti, *Surreal Woman with a Shell That Wraps Her Face.* AdobeStock.com #396768583.

Library of Congress Cataloging-in-Publication Data
A catalog record for this book is available from the Library of Congress.

British Library Cataloguing-in-Publication Data
A catalog record for this book is available from the British Library.

The authorized representative in the EU for product safety and compliance is Mare-Nostrum Group.
Email: gpsr@mare-nostrum.co.uk
Physical address: Mare-Nostrum Group B.V., Mauritskade 21D, 1091 GC Amsterdam, The Netherlands

For my mother, and for Lou

CONTENTS

A BROOM TO REMOVE THE DUST

Immediately upon exiting the elevator, you will first turn right. Make a second, tight right into a glorified alcove dubbed ECT WAITING. The walls will be a pale mint green, so pale it's almost white—but also, not at all white. You'll know because the ceiling will be very white, the chairs cheap pleather gray and faux light birch, the contrast clear. There will be an old-fashioned telephone on one of three matching side tables, the one nearest the entry to the alcove and directly underneath the wall-mounted television set, which will be off. The phone will be black, the numbered buttons gray and punchable. There will be a laminated sign above the phone requesting patients to please call this number (followed by a number) to alert staff of arrival.

The first time, you will read this number to your mother as she dials, stand above her silver head, her hair a squarish cloud of fluff above a black and white striped t-shirt. You'll try, in other words, to make this easier. You will notice some things now, and others later. Later, for example: the black lockbox on the wall beneath the sign, purposes unknown. Later, the slim crucifix that hangs against the center wall between two dull, mismatched, matted prints in frames (scenes of Paris, windowsills, *boulangerie*), none of them lined up exactly, each a little off. Later, one slight desk lamp, decorative in curlicue wrought iron. Inexplicable beneath the halogen-bathed halls in this unit, open only until noon, three days a week.

You'll learn to notice these and other things as you log time. Learn to recognize the other faces, bodies, here beside you. Everybody comes and goes, the schedule changes, new faces appear. Some you'll wind up talking to, others not. Either way, this is where you'll wait, three days each week for two weeks and then two days for the third week. You'll sit and read and look and think and drink your coffee.

Down the hall, your mother will lie back on a gurney to be seized.

~~~

A medically induced seizure is a mystery, even to the shrinks. That's what my mom, at sixty-seven, persists in calling them: *the shrinks*. That it works against depression is not only proven but impressive—a success rate, according to researchers at Johns Hopkins, higher than any other single treatment or psychiatric medication. Controversial and uncertain (not to the *if* but to the *why* of its effectiveness), seizure therapy is just that: therapy. Not torture, not "shock treatment," and most certainly no ecstatic paroxysm of pain or pleasure.

In Cole Swensen's translation of *Now, Now, Louison*, Jean Frémon's "portrait in motion" of the late Louise Bourgeois, Frémon renders Bourgeois's inner dialogue, considering the experience of bodies sent into hysterics: "In a seizure, the body becomes a sculpture, the eyes popping out, the wrists twisted outward, the ankles angling in."

These past two midsummer evenings, each spent in a downtown hotel in Spokane near the hospital, I've devoured Frémon's novella—two nights, two bars, each episode an effort to assuage the
~~~

neck and shoulder tension, the worry and relief that saturate these days begun at ECT WAITING. I stumbled on the book by chance back in March, just weeks after getting a rendition of Bourgeois's *Spiral Woman* figure tattooed on my right triceps. Though I bought a copy eagerly, not only for the subject but also for the aesthetics of the physical object itself (smooth, white, slender, the title in classic Courier along the spine), I took until this week to crack it open—and once begun, I couldn't stop. Couldn't unsee the parallels between this story, this woman's concerns, and my own at this exact and trying moment.

The moment in question is July 2019. I am thirty-four years old and staring down my second year as a full-time college writing instructor, the first a singular blur of English 101 composition papers and early morning commutes and attempts to revise my graduate school lifestyle—of late nights drinking and writing and arguing with poet friends down at the bar, of predetermined reading lists and manuscript deadlines and minimal teaching loads—into something resembling stable adulthood. At the same time, I am living across town from my mother and her distinct accumulations: of wingtip oxford shoes and too-pink lipsticks, striped t-shirts and bottles of cheap, sweet Riesling, fresh flowers and French bread and stagnant sadness and a host of health concerns spinning out from a series of surgeries and cancer treatments in the years surrounding her separation from my father.

It is a moment of high tension: a hot northern Idaho summer, bright and brittle and dry. My mother's sporadic depression has, in recent months, become acute, her body, a constant liability. In response, my own body tightens inward, muscle and organ gripping a disordered anxiety I've yet to recognize for what it is.

Amid this difficulty, this pinching fear, Bourgeois's fascination with the body—its geometry, its rotundities—has come to fascinate me almost as much as her life and work. Ever since my friend Sarah sent me a postcard depicting one of Bourgeois's midcentury pieces from the Tate Modern in London—blue, abstract, watercolor, untitled, eyes peering out into somewhere between two wet leaves, a cascade of hair or a veil tumbling like extravagantly long lashes beneath a semi-obfuscated blue gaze—I've found myself curious, drawn in by the peculiarity and independence of her strokes, her bodily awareness, her iterative attention to the little oddities (spiders, breasts, cellular arrangements) of this: our animality, our life. The tattoo idea was born of obsession and superficial research; but the tattoo itself, the getting of it, transformed into a commitment of sorts—to Bourgeois, to her interests, to understanding her art and myself, in parallel. I admire, even envy, certain aspects of her life: her creative audacity and determined psychological investigation, her independent approach to the work of making and remaking, asking questions, chasing down her loves in every shape and stroke.

"To create something where nothing had been before, that's sculpting," writes Frémon (as Bourgeois). Such is a tattoo. Such is a seizing body, headless and suspended from a string. Such is a synaptic flash.

~~~

The first time my mother and I went to Providence Hospital, an affiliate of Sacred Heart, was for mom's electroconvulsive therapy registration and intake appointment with the psychiatrist, Dr. R—an artfully coiffed South Asian man with respectable gray streaks in his dark hair, unscuffed leather shoes, and a pair of trendy translucent acetate glasses. I recall, despite my worry and the freezing temperatures inside the air-conditioned corridors, my summer dress a paltry defense against hospital AC, a blip of envy—envy, and appreciation. Such style, in these otherwise austere and empty, dull gray halls.

I was also admittedly seeking distraction. The appointment worried me. That my mother was struggling, that she needed help, was clear; but after decades of watching her move impulsively from fad diets to plastic surgery, from uppers to downers, from
~~~

yoga to Zumba to Botox, I was skeptical of her sudden insistence that ECT was the answer. Never one for moderation, Mom tended to dramatize her symptoms and seek extreme treatments. Quite frankly, I didn't trust her judgment. In assessing Dr. R, sartorial sensibilities aside, I was looking for a mirror—of my concerns, of my cautiousness. And perhaps, though I wouldn't have admitted it then, of my tendency to patronize my mother when she seemed, to me, verging on irrationality.

Dr. R asked direct questions. His eyes behind the acetate a steady presence; a comfort. I began to think he would suggest a tiered approach, something less drastic than my imagined version of electricity. But my mother's bid for treatment was approved. She was scheduled for six days out.

Leaving, we passed a wall of windows facing what seemed, at first, to be a courtyard. Fig-tree leaves, heavy green, and unripe teardrops in brilliant neon. Our ECT nurse and guide back to the elevator explained, in broken English (she is Russian), that the tree belonged to the house that still sits in the middle of the campus. Private, historic, twenty-five rooms; satin wallpaper and late Victorian fixtures (the house was built in 1906); gracious fig-leaf green and painted wood and white and all of it just sitting there: a thing of beauty, sprawling and eccentric, amid so much concrete, sickness, skybridge-fraught expansion. The owner, an immigrant herself and something of a Spokane matriarch, had dug in her heels. Refused to sell. Now she is survived by several children, and the daughter—in her seventies—has followed suit.

The nurse laughed, said that Mary, the elderly lady who had owned the house, used to make extra money by charging for parking, renting out the lawn. Twenty-five cents per hour. That was 1947. In an article from the local newspaper, the *Spokesman-Review*, published in 2011, Mary's daughter Dorothy tells reporter Stephanie Pettit of a nun from Sacred Heart who used to visit Mary nearly once per week, always asking the same question: didn't Mary think it was God's will that she should sell the house to the hospital?

"Mother would say that no, God hadn't spoken to her yet about that," Dorothy tells Pettit.

I find this article, and several others, in the wake of this passing conversation with the nurse, and on the eve of mother's first appointment with adult psychiatry at Providence. Mom is upstairs in our hotel room watching TV. I am downstairs in the lobby bar, sipping a martini and drafting syllabi and lesson plans in between Googling "ECT," "Sacred Heart," "Dr. R." I'm equal parts intrigued by the story of Mary's Place (that's what the house is called now) and anxious to quell my anxieties about the next day's treatment.

On the hour-and-a-half drive from Moscow, Idaho, to Spokane, Washington, my mother told me all about the Bible study series she's been watching on her iPhone when she can't go back to sleep at night. A newly confirmed Catholic, she's already having doubts about matters of tradition, confession, and sainthood—and finds herself falling back on the evangelical Protestant ideologies that used to give her so much comfort.

"I feel like such a dilettante sometimes, changing my mind, questioning," she says, leaning back into her seat as my Subaru Impreza rumbles over hills and under bridges through the green and gold Palouse. "Skip"—the born-again Bible study leader's name is Skip, a former surfer, tan, with such a perfect swoop of sun-kissed hair—"on the one hand, Skip really tears Mary to pieces. Says the way the Catholics speak of her is absolute idolatry. On the other, the only real recorded vision of Mary *herself* coming down to say anything to anyone was just 'build a cathedral here; I want the people to know my son.'"

"That doesn't sound so bad," I offer, adjusting the radio volume dial down a notch. I spent ten years at Catholic school, after a Lutheran confirmation at age seven. My mom and I were confirmed together. Despite my current unaffiliated status and extreme institutional skepticism, I don't think that she's crazy to believe.

"Hardly self-aggrandizing on her part, right?" I venture.

"Well, yeah," says Mom. She trails off, reaches for the half-full bag of Kettle salt and vinegar potato chips shoved into the inside passenger-side cupholder.

Not long after, she is back to all of this: the saints, and what Skip has to say, and how is one supposed to ever know what to believe. Every drive, back and forth, we loop.

~~~

Tonight, you wait for storms. Lightning, thunder—something to disrupt this aching heat. They say the storms will come by midnight, maybe. Bulbous clouds and wind. Electrical disturbances, most welcome.

Seizure, in the medical, biological sense, is defined as an abnormal electrical discharge in the brain. It is also, of course, defined as a sudden attack or possession taking—either violent or, in certain contexts, via legal means and procedural action. ECT, from what you can ascertain, seems like the latter: a legal, procedural, consensual taking, for a period of roughly thirty to sixty seconds, of the patient's brain. This conquest is neither violent nor vampiric, at least from the purview of the attending psychiatrist, anesthesiologist, and nurse. It would seem, on the contrary, to be thoughtful—cheerful, even—as well as closely monitored and altogether careful. In observing the patient prep and intake process over these past weeks, you find the word *paternal* coming to mind—perhaps in part because you're preparing to teach Eula Biss's *On Immunity: An Inoculation* this semester, and are thus filled with thoughts on medicine, metaphor, and culture (not to mention talk of vampires). Plus, both the attending psychiatrists—Dr. R and another, younger, doctor, Dr. C—are men.

On the one hand, you trust these doctors well enough. You do not find their maleness, in this context, predatory. Then again, the ideas and images you conjure of the vampire's victim and that of the woman in contorted ecstasy—whether from divine visitation, or sexual pleasure, or electrical disturbance—are not at all dissimilar.
~~~

To be seized, it seems, is a much-anticipated fate: one that's planted deep within so many of your metaphors and monster myths alike. Your ways of looking at and wanting, fearing, and believing in the world. Your ways, even, of contending with desire—the tricky politics of sex, of bodies, and of wanting in a world fraught with so much wrong and horror that the very urge to be caught up against the teeth of want, to be held there, powerless, ecstatic, feels insensitive at best, and sick at worst.

Tonight, you are up too late. This, despite the long day, despite your mother's 7:45 a.m. appointment with the black rotary phone and gray pleather chairs in ECT WAITING earlier this morning, despite the drive home afterward, despite unpacking and dishes and emails and chores. But you can't sleep. You're waiting for the storm.

Eventually, you go to bed. Leave the window cracked.

Near midnight, having drifted off, you wake again to an insistent and repeating "clink" against the windowpane. The sound is so repetitive, so regimented in its tones, you can't help but assume (in that singular state of mostly-asleepness) that it's something mechanized: a neighbor, a timer, a car battery gone rogue. That this clink, in fact, is rain, takes longer than usual to register. You must wake again, hours later, to its smell: summer rain, wet and heat commingled with a sudden breeze, pushed right through the dirty screen into your room and then your nostrils, suddenly. Beautiful and soft, and likewise startling.

Once upon a time, you had lovers. Sometimes, lovers who would wake you up with kiss and touch and seizure, soft and quiet and adroit. Sometimes, sleeping bodies are like sculptures: seizure by soft hands and lips might wake a marble frieze into new life—of ecstasy, or fear. It's hard to ascertain, at times, which sense is which. Something in this muggy gray-sky nighttime, in the smell and soft of 2 a.m., makes you want that thing you've lately given up. The sense and grip of ecstasy you can feel all by yourself: all you need is some electricity. A pair of batteries and soft-worn crimson sheets between the motor and your naked skin. Neck kicked back, wrists gripped tight, ankles firm to ground your feet into the mattress plush.

~~~

The mystery of electroconvulsive therapy is partnered with that surrounding depression. Because researchers and psychiatrists are still pinning down the exact cause and function of depression, the ways in which extreme electrical stimulus to the brain can and will alleviate symptoms remain, likewise, unclear.

A seizure is the most a brain can take, point blank. This may cause the dampened-down emotional barometer that many patients feel from ECT. Recent studies (again, drawing on research from Johns Hopkins) have begun to examine whether ECT may work, in fact, by altering the very structure of the synapse. Such changes would, as ECT has shown, impact everything from memory to cognition to emotional register. Results, however, remain inconclusive.

Meanwhile, my mother has been "zapped," as she calls it, six times. Her memory does lapse. Her balance and awareness also lapse, as do her taste buds. Vision shifts, turning into what she calls "HD," as in high definition (this began after the very first appointment, in the hotel room, with an HDTV screen and Mom, with such a brutal headache, hooked to watching something, anything, even as the HD format made her feel unsteady and confused; it hasn't left her since). During Mom's registration appointment, Dr. R informed me that I may well notice changes before she does—so I've been watching. She is sweet and generous and far less angry than she was; but also, she is tired and "just out of it," as she has texted me over and over.

"Everything feels weird" is something of a canned reply at this point, any time I write to ask how she is doing.

It's Sunday night. We're back in Spokane for the last two treatments—that is, the final two of the initial eight. Call time is
~~~

tomorrow, 8:45 a.m. For now, my mom is tucked in, listening to surfer Skip unpack the Book of Acts on YouTube; I am at a nearby bar, wine and salted pub mix and a book in hand, watching rain deluge the heat-baked city streets downtown. Today was it: the long-awaited storm, in earnest. Bold thunder; sky-wide lightning; sudden, violent, heavy rain—flooding gutters, prompting squeals and hollers up and down the street. Earlier, walking back from various errands, I found myself caught up in it—running, laughing, helpless in the face of so much wet and torrent, feet soaked, legs soaked. Uncontrollable relief, after a week of such relentless heat.

Last week, Sarah and I attended a small but significant exhibit of Louise Bourgeois's later works. The exhibit, titled *Ode to Forgetting*, has been visiting the art museum at the state university campus where I teach. Somehow—burdened, I believe, by my own sense that I needed to allot the proper time for reverence, reflection, not a hurried detour on the busy days that find me intermittently on campus in the summer—I'd been putting off my visit. I am, admittedly, (and much as my own mother would love me to forget), my father's daughter: a master procrastinator. This meant Sarah and I caught the show on its penultimate day.

After her first two treatments, my mother complained most acutely of disorientation. The headaches had been swiftly fixed—simply a matter of preemptive medication, hospital-grade Tylenol, administered before each treatment. Confusion, though, remained: she found herself unsteady ("wobbly," in her words), not sure what was going on at times, or how to navigate the crosshairs of an otherwise uncomplicated prospect like a gas station mini-mart or grocery store checkout. When we returned to Providence, and she explained her confusion, the attending psychiatrist switched her procedure from bilateral to unilateral application, adjusting the electrical disturbance from both sides of the brain to only one. According to Dr. Reti at Johns Hopkins (no known relation to my mother's Dr. R), this is a verified approach for mitigating short-term memory loss when undergoing ECT. Rather than applying leads to both sides of the forehead, the unilateral approach involves one front and one side lead—and, from my perspective, a drastic difference in my mother's sense of comfort and confusion after treatment.

Bourgeois's mother died when she was young. Louise, the artist, loved her mother with a fierceness that perhaps only single daughters (privy to the misdemeanors and neglect of fathers) truly can. I do not mean, in writing this, to say my father was neglectful. He was, however, often absent, and unsuited to my mother, and vice versa. On that count, they agree. He has since moved on, reengaged himself. Mom and I, in all of this, are on our own.

Frémon writes, as Bourgeois, of the stricture Louise felt after her mother died, as her father bought her frilly clothes and found her monied suitors. Not long after, equipped with an artistic eye and an astute weaving acumen, she ran. She married but kept her father's name. She memorialized her mother in countless shapes and sizes as a spider—protective, watchful, caring, clever, black against a backdrop of bright white. In the end, she, too, likewise remained her father's daughter.

Looking at Bourgeois's prints and drawings and multimedia textiles, I can see it: the tension and the truth of this split self, of her motherlove and fatherlikeness. How she interrogates the intersections of her past and present: Saint Sebastian as a woman, headless, heavy-breasted, and beset with arrows. Spider after spider after spider—some slumped into corners of what seems to be a single room. A multimedia piece entitled *The Guilty Girl Is Fragile*: "The triangular figure rests on a single point and can easily fall down" reads the artist's statement. "Her guilt has nothing to do with religion."

I see, and I can understand, and I am happy for the ink along my upper right-side triceps. For my tattooer's rendition of Bourgeois's *Spiral Woman*—her head all flowing mane and Mona Lisa smile, her arms and legs cartoonish, her body larval and rotund—as a reminder of the themes that drew Bourgeois to the spiral figure in the first place. And from her attraction, mine.

Freedom and control. Freedom and control. Turning, turning, turning.

Writing as Bourgeois, describing her sculpture of a body in hysterics, Frémon says, "I'll suspend the arcing body by a cable attached to its navel and let it turn slowly around. Appeasement. Joy in eternal gyration. Head gone. Out of control. To each their own orgasm."

~~~

Your mother's last Spokane appointment was on Tuesday. Today, it's Saturday. Tonight, you meet her at a local restaurant in downtown Moscow for wine and fresh caprese salad—ripe heirloom tomatoes in their season, oil- and balsamic-drenched, a little basil and a ball of fresh-made cheese. All you could taste were those tomatoes in the oil, richness and salt, flavor and abandon. A summer blessing.

Before the tomatoes, you walk up to the restaurant patio and see your mother from behind, her silver hair, her trademark black and white stripes. When your order arrives, the two of you clink glasses: your prosecco to her Lambrusco. ("Not what I got so sick on all those years ago, is it?" she chuckles to the server, when asked how the wine is holding up.) You toast to the completion of her treatments, eight in all, and drink to better days ahead. For now, she is still tired and (as she says) "just weird." Her sense of taste still off, her energy reduced. You see it, but you also see a shift in how she seems to view the world. Sometimes her eyes are vacant, and that worries you because she's always been so sharp. Other times she smiles in the sweetest way—tonight, for instance, watching a woman with a dog on her lap at a neighboring table, how the tiny dog wanted to chase a fly, how the woman wraps her napkin around the dog's small, spotted, black-and-white-furred body to soothe him.

"He must be the best dog in the world," your mom says, watching, the edges of a smile creeping against the borders of her eyes, her lips. "So close to pizza, and he isn't even sniffing it or anything."
~~~

A month ago, the sight of a dog might have sent your mother into a fit of tears and anguish—missing all your old family pets, lamenting her little apartment, its restrictions. Tonight, she looks at this small dog with love that feels so purely of the moment, so appreciative of life. It gives you hope.

Saint Bernadette—the French girl, the one the Virgin Mary singled out for visitation, the one whose visions eventually established Lourdes as a principal pilgrimage place for Catholics in the western world—offered (at least according to Wikipedia), when criticized or questioned, this frank and tidy statement regarding her visions: "The Virgin used me as a broom to remove the dust. When the work is done, the broom is put behind the door again." While you have no idea where your mother will come down regarding Mary, or the Catholic church, or Skip, or any of the ways and means by which guilt might be used to push her into corners, you do have some idea that she is better off after these past three weeks, after Providence and ECT WAITING. It's tough, because you worry—still, you worry—and, as you and she and all the shrinks and doctors can attest, ECT changes the brain itself. It does not change the circumstances of one's life.

In other words: your mom will still be aging and alone, at sixty-seven. She will still be often tired, often parked in front of TCM movie marathons (like tonight, which is Errol Flynn night, a fact that—because you are your mother's daughter, too, and watched these films with her as you grew up—prompts much discussion: of Flynn and Flora Robeson and Olivia de Havilland, of the overlapping casts of films like *The Adventures of Robin Hood, The Sea Hawk*, and *Captain Blood*, and what else was being made each year, and how the plotlines, likewise, intersect). She may very well stay tired; may very well still want to travel in theory, stay at home in practice. You cannot know.

As for you? Your time spent pacing back and forth across the bridge between the Main and Children's Hospitals at Providence, looking out the windows at the figs and leaves and white and greenery of Mary's Place; or drinking Thomas Hammer coffee in the ER coffee shop you didn't even know was there until week two; or making conversations with a mother, then a social worker, then a husband under too-bright lights, under the auspices of ECT WAITING, the filtered atmosphere of such a spare and label-ridden space, in fact, facilitating openness in ways you never would have guessed at . . . what of you? What of that? What of this?

~~~

"*The Guilty Girl* . . . is an example of Bourgeois incorporating personal fabrics into her printmaking practice." So reads the museum information plaque beside the Guilty Girl herself: a devilishly relatable pair of disgruntled, crossed eyes, housed in an upside-down red triangle of a face, printed "on the artist's own undergarment," a delicate and gauzy white slip. I took a photograph of Sarah, standing to the left of the red-faced Guilty Girl. Sarah is standing in a corner, wearing red pants and a black t-shirt, examining the red and black portrait of the artist's aging hand; I am examining Sarah as juxtaposed with said hand and said Guilty Girl, myself dressed all in black. Sarah takes my picture with one of Bourgeois's iconic, headless, heavy-breasted, black and white Saint Sebastian prints mere minutes later, and I look back at the photograph to make sure I do, in fact, recall what I was wearing. We could not have planned it any better.

Bourgeois's hybrid works in *Ode to Forgetting* include many instances of personal fabric—literally, as in pieces of her clothing, or metaphorically, as in language drawn from her diaries and journals—arranged against the type of steady, regimented, black-and-white-striped lines most often found on music composition paper. At the time she made these pieces, she was in her late eighties (or older), repurposing and recombining elements and pieces of a life, a self, a body. Holding on? Perhaps. Letting go? Perhaps that, too.
~~~

I look back at the photographs I took at the exhibit, as well as those that Sarah took of me. Photographs of art and space and text, of black and white and color. Looking, I recall the way I'd noticed, once, out of the corner of my eye, that she was holding up her iPhone as if to take a picture, and how I'd tried, in that moment, to steady my body, restrict it—cinch in my belly with a breath, hold my shoulders back—and still, despite my hyper self-awareness, failed. The photo itself, all the evidence one needs of what a t-shirt dress does and does not hide about the body of a thirty-something woman, in profile, leaning back, at the end of yet another wine-filled summer. Rotundities, geometry. The dress was loose; my body, from the outside, thoroughly unsculpted. All that shaping, seizing, came from me: my sense of what I ought to do, controlled and without pleasure.

ON BECOMING

I was conceived in San Francisco, in the springtime. It was afternoon, I'm told. There was sunshine and a bottle of Andre's Brut. As my mother tells it, sex between my parents was quite rare. The cheap champagne, in other words, was a necessity of my becoming.

Looking down at my fingertips, I see the shape of my pinky nail. These nails are my father's nails: oval-square, too broad to be delicate. I am at once an anomaly and a patchwork. An amalgam of two people's proclivities and appetites, love affairs and traumas. What they ate and drank and inhaled and touched and thought and read and heard before and during the making of my body.

Conception is defined as a design or plan. It is an invention. The act or power of forming notions. The Middle English root comes from the Latin for "concept": the way in which something is perceived or regarded. But sometimes the plan comes after the conceiving itself. The design, an afterthought. When it comes to having a baby, I think of conception as a tone shift on the psychosomatic register: from a vague fear, perhaps, or a long-held fantasy, into something material.

~~~

Medical Record

Mother
April 1984

Case Summary
She is thirty-three years old. She wants kids but isn't exactly trying. She has been married for two years. She is beginning to have second thoughts. Like when he comes home late again after softball with the partners, after pizza and pitchers of beer, then turns on the news or flips to the sports page while they lie beside each other in bed. When she begins to feel invisible.

Before this, she was the co-director at a progressive preschool in the Marina District. She liked it, even though at least half the kids were, as she often said, "spoiled little shits" with rich actors for parents. She loves kids. She wants to make a difference.

Now she has quit smoking, stopped using cocaine, but still drinks (mostly wine, mostly white). She has had one abortion. She has been raped twice—the first time by the man with the knife, and the second time by the man who was her boyfriend, the time she wasn't sure if she could call a rape until much later. That is what she told the lady lawyer over that one dinner in Los Angeles, what she told the judge at the preliminary hearing, what she told her husband, what she tells herself. What she will one day tell her daughter. So much depends on definitions. She doesn't know it yet, but several of these definitions will later be shaped and reshaped in court by that same lady lawyer; by millions of women, including her daughter, on social media. She doesn't know it yet, but her role in testifying against the serial rapist who waited near bus stops, watching for women, would help lead that lady lawyer eventually to challenge O. J. Simpson, Dodi Fayed, Bill Cosby, and Harvey Weinstein.
~~~

Medication History

The depression of her teen years is at bay. No more living at home, nineteen years old, taking pulls off Dad's handle of Gordon's and eating hot dogs and head lettuce in the meantime, Bing Crosby and Bob Hope bantering on TV. No more sense of failure, inability to even throw a goddamn pot in ceramics class without crying.

Back then, she shoveled clinically dosed vitamins—B, C, D, E. Now, nothing prescribed. Not even birth control. She prefers the diaphragm to condoms. Why trust a man when she can control the situation herself? She still takes vitamins: B-Complex, C, E, and A. Everything that once worked like magic on her broken skin. She eats better now—cabbage, broccoli, tofu, sprouts—but still, she takes them. Out of obedience. Out of caution.

She doesn't know it yet, but the day will come when she can't eat any of these things without causing chaos inside her body. When she will be forced to trade in most raw and even cooked vegetables, beans, and grains for canned asparagus and French bread, tomato soup and white rice. When a series of rectal and intestinal surgeries followed by devastating radiation and chemotherapy treatments for a tiny carcinoma will leave her with intermittent adhesions that result in blockages and inflammation and send her to the ER with intestinal obstruction more than half a dozen times.

For now, though, that is all in the future. As undetermined as the weather.

What else? HPV in her late twenties. A history of antidepressants. The drinking. She never tells her doctors just how much.

Medical History

Her own mother's stats look good on paper. On the outside: slim, active, a regular golfer, a talented painter. She made bacon for her husband and canned pear salad for herself, framed her paintings on the walls and got her hair done every week. "Ate like a bird," she always said. Inside, though, she is a nervous wreck. It will be fifteen years or so before the strokes, then the seeds of dementia spring up inside her brain and take root. And her mother's mother: a medical calamity. Dead in her thirties from botched surgeries and gangrene, saddled before that with an abusive, philandering artist husband. The one time he came back to see her, her son opened the door and said, "Who wants to know?" Her son was five. His estranged father punched him in the jaw.

On her father's side: so-called Black Irish, at least according to family lore. Bootleggers and horse thieves. Uncle Mike lost two fingers in a factory accident. Aunt Ina always spoiled the children. Her father had been handsome; now he is a red-faced alcoholic with a bloated nose. Five gin martinis a day, chased with a Snickers from his stash in the living-room end table. A bigot, a pilot, and a charmer.

Sometimes she looks through family albums and takes inventory. Her father is a rogue, her mother is a beauty. She can appreciate the irony: that, in all her baby pictures—the round face, the dark pupils, the winking grin, the shock of black curls—it's her father she sees staring back.

~~~

What are bodies if not composite things? And, if so, then perhaps my body is made of air and smoke and anger. Of gin and hot dogs and head lettuce. Or maybe none of these. There are so many pieces to choose from. So many strands of code to be activated, queued up, or stashed away.

Epigenetics is defined as the study of changes in organisms caused by modification of gene expression rather than alteration of the genetic code itself. In other words, there are the genes I've got, and then the misfits among them. Genes that get turned on or turned off—depending, perhaps, on what I eat, or what my mother ate, or how little her own mother had to fill her belly during the Depression; how much I was hugged as a child, or how much my father was bullied on the schoolyard, or how my father's mother did or did not show affection to her husband. How my own playground
~~~

pleasures and hungers and fears—the speed, for instance, with which I flung myself from parallel bars in the second grade, racing my classmates in what we dubbed "the bar game," utterly unconcerned for my own safety, wrapped up in the thrill of the chase, or the openness with which I'd ask to taste my best friends' chips or cookies at lunch because I never got to have these things at home—might change as I grew older.

Developmental cognitive neuroscientists have found that human characteristics—both physical and psychological—result from interactions between biological molecules and their contexts. Contexts, as in the environment: South Pasadena or West Hollywood or San Francisco or a bayside refinery town where Jack London used to frequent the brothels and soldiers kept camels in the sandstone barracks; fluoridated tap water or lines of cocaine or Andre's Brut or carob-flavored Vitasoy; B-vitamin deficiency or post-traumatic stress disorder or plain old anxiety.

Contexts, as in the other half of the story.

I'm trying to understand this. It's a tricky subject, and my science is rusty. And because I am in the first year of my MFA program in creative writing but also taking an ecocriticism class, because, at thirty, I've been out of school for more than ten years, because I'm still fighting off my first-semester imposter syndrome and my workshop professor is unexpectedly well versed in physics and neuroscience and the study of inherited trauma, I'm nervous. Determined, as I always have been in academics, to excel; to figure this shit out. So I go to the library, go to Wikipedia, engage in rigorous Googling. I even finish most of David S. Moore's surprisingly readable, refreshingly narrative book on the subject, *The Developing Genome: An Introduction to Behavioral Epigenetics*. And ultimately what I gather is this: that contrary to the biological determinism most scientists have ascribed to for decades, DNA alone does not fate us. Rather, it is the white space, the potential, the realm above the gene (*epi* is the Greek root meaning "above," "on," or "on top of") that clinches things.

Epigenetic changes occur in phenotype (observable traits) as opposed to genotype (the inherited genetic makeup of the cell). In its simplest iteration, this change transforms the cells present in an embryo into all the different cells necessary to build a body: skin cells, brain cells, red-blood cells, white-blood cells. The process works by way of methylation, in which genes are codified for specific tasks. Codified, as in named, systematized, structured. Unknowns, pinned down at last.

Throughout fetal development, methylation is key to the evolution of a sperm and egg into a cluster of cells. From there, the process transforms that cluster into a tadpole, and then that tadpole into something resembling a tiny human with arms and curled fingers and legs wrapped tight against its chest. But there is something else. Something beyond the scaffolding, the designation of helixes, that occurs in the womb. There is the movement of methyl groups that occurs later, after birth: in response to diet, or toxicity, or trauma, or even affection. There is the question of inheritance—from a mother, or a father, or perhaps even a grandmother—of those things that live above the genes, outside the twists of code.

~~~

Medical Record

Father
April 1984

Case Summary
He is twenty-nine years old. He wants kids, absolutely. He wants to do it all right: the ring, the wife, the woman who makes him laugh while they watch *The Jerk* on cable, each cradling the phone receiver against one ear in their respective apartments, or while they split peanut-butter fudge sundaes at Loard's Ice Cream after dinner at the all-you-can-eat pizza buffet.
~~~

He grew up an Eagle Scout. He grew up incensed by injustice. He remembers the way his mother walked through the grocery store pushing her cart with her nose in the air, as if no one else needed a path through the aisle. Or the way the twins down the street, Bob and Ron Carter, turned and ran when he came to their aid on the baseball diamond, leaving him to the mercy of the bullying McBride brothers. He was nine. He didn't know how to fight. He simply needed to do something about it—the sense of impending violence, injustice. The mismatch of the hulking McBrides and the scrawny Carters. He's always felt a compulsion to protect the underdog.

Medication History

Not much. He rarely gets sick. But whenever he does, he's down for the count, sleeping fourteen hours straight. He doesn't take vitamins. At twenty-nine, he's still tall and lean. The arthritic knees, the trouble with his eyes . . . all of that is yet to come.

Medical History

Just this knee pain that flares up when he plays softball now, or basketball. He used to play basketball fine. Used to run, fast. But bad knees are in his blood: his mother, his father, his older sister. All of them, besides his brother, will end up having surgery. All of them, except his two sisters, will end up having skin cancer. He will, too, although he doesn't know it yet.

Right now, it's hard to tell any of this—not just with him, but within his family. What might be real, and what is not quite real. His mother has turned hypochondriac. Every time he speaks with her, she's got some kind of virus. You'd never know it to look at her: nearly six feet tall, blond, and heavy-limbed, the type to love and resent with equal measures of ferocity. His father is, on the other hand, already stooped: back round, nose beakish. His father is (and was and will be until death) the sweetest man in the world.

~~~
~~~

How to narrow down context? How to understand the possibilities? Consider the Latin roots *con*—"together"—and *texere*—"to weave." Or the Late Middle English term denoting the construction of a text.

I said earlier that origins define us. But perhaps I need to unpack that word—*define*—a little more. I'm thinking of those magnetic poetry kits. I'm picturing a box with a set number of words. The scope of the thing begins to make sense: *define*, as in the Latin *definire*—"to set bounds to." There are the words that we get, and then the ideas we can use those words to express.

In those early autumn weeks of my first year of graduate school, I went to a party at a fellow student's apartment. On-campus housing, too-bright kitchen lights, a bathroom door that didn't lock. People disappearing every now and then to get high in the upstairs bedroom. Everyone else cohered in the kitchen, moving together and then apart, clustering now around the table littered with open bags of Doritos and plastic trays of Safeway five-layer dip, now around the fridge well stocked with PBR, Rainier, soda, a few bottles of cheap prosecco. On the fridge, scattered pieces from a magnetic poetry kit. One by one, creative writing students taking their turn. Adhering the clustered strips to that humming Kenmore or GE or Maytag or Frigidaire (the model, I don't remember; the model, in this instance, immaterial).

Despite a boyfriend back at home in Los Angeles, I had a crush among the crowd. At least, I worried that I might have one—it was so new, I was so new, all this newness a perpetual buzz in my chest. Perhaps I simply had a crush on this strange new life, this long-deferred return to academia, to literature and art. I was living once again in that freshly rediscovered heat and thrum: of strangers and smiles, of intellectual banter as the default mode for flirtation, of glances and allusion and suggestion. Waiting to see who would speak too closely, who would suddenly disappear, and with whom. Watching that ego-fueled chess match on the refrigerator door: all of us writers, vying, flexing. Watching letters dance and shift beneath each poet's hands, new clusters to make us laugh or smirk depending on whose fingers were in charge, on who was trying to avoid conversation, on how many cans of PBR were left in the fridge.

I understand that science metaphors are tricky. I see how hard it is—to catch all the pieces, all the complexity, in the tidy pocket of a single image. But when the very word—*epigenetics*—is itself a metaphor, how can one help but try? Help but plumb and stretch to make the fabric fit? I recall those magnetic poems on the fridge, the shitty beer, the noise of the party. Later, I will look back at that time—before I knew that everything would change, that my boyfriend back in Los Angeles and I would break up within months, that I would become involved with at least several of the other men present at that party in one way or another, that none of it would last outside the confines of that heady, booze-laden, three-year graduate program. And suddenly I get it: that environment is everything. That the power to define, in this case, is inexact beyond the biological molecules themselves.

So do our environments, then, hold the key to what happens? And, if so, how far back do I go? Do I start with my birth at Alta Bates in Berkeley, California? Or with the refinery town where I grew up, charming main street and waterfront on one side of the bay and belching smokestacks on the other? Do I look to my mother's childhood in the suburbs outside Los Angeles? To the smog banks and borrowed water and Manson murders and phony smiles and haunted bus stops that mapped her sense of the city? Do I look to my father's life in Fort Wayne, Indiana? Swimming in the reservoir, smoking ditch weed, loving snow but feeling, deep down, a tug toward the west, toward California?

I could go on. Recall every myth, branch, and bloodline. Claim the Black Irish Wards with their storied thirst and fear of famine; the Porters, pretty Brits with blond curls and perfect noses; the Scottish Gibsons with their long thick legs and clannish loyalty; the Vestervelts, supposedly of the Dutch West India Company, slave traders and colonizers. I could even learn, as I will later, just how much of this is fiction. How family history—and, with it, what we think we know about environments, about our origins, about ourselves—gets warped in the retelling. How none of us—my mother, my father, my poet friends, myself—are reliable narrators.

~~~

Medical Record

Daughter
April 2016

Case Summary
She is thirty-one years old. She doesn't smoke. Not cigarettes (except for a few times, here and there), and not pot (anymore, though sometimes she wishes she still did). The only time she smoked a cigarette for real—real as in she properly inhaled—she spent two hours on the floor of a dingy dorm-hall bathroom. That was in 2004. She was eighteen. The many times afterward that she smoked weed, in her early twenties, felt euphoric. Then euphoria subsided, turned to palpitations, paranoia. Years later, listening to a *Fresh Air* interview with Steve Martin, she will learn that this is a common response. That once the paranoia sets in, it can turn a person off from THC for good. She will learn that she and Steve Martin have this in common, and it will bring her minor comfort.

These days, she drinks (mostly wine; sometimes beer or whiskey or gin). She tries to be moderate. She does not always succeed. She knows that weakness runs in her blood.

At thirty-one, she might want kids, or she might not. Since beginning graduate school, she errs toward the latter. She resents the pressure to choose. She has only just started her new life, her possible new career, and wants to imagine herself with the same seeming limitlessness of her twenty-something female peers, or the
~~~

same luxury of time to wallow in heartache as her forty-something male friends.

She would, at this age, be considered grown up by any standard definition of the word, but she doesn't feel like it. Not often. Especially not when it comes to romantic relationships. She has only had one boyfriend; two lovers; six sexual partners. One date most folks would call "blind." At least twenty more that, looking back, feel blinder. Nine years since losing her virginity. Nine days, in this sudden neon springtime green, since having sex for the first time with a new partner after breaking up with her ex. Five years left, give or take, to become a mother—that is, without societal warnings and added risk. Maybe twenty-five years, give or take, since she's known—somehow, deep down—that sex would be a source of trouble.

She has never had an abortion. Never been pregnant. Never been raped—at least, never with any hint of threat or violence. It's the question of consent, though—consent and assault—that trips her up. So much depends on definitions. Consent as in permission, allowance, agreement. Assault, as in hit, strike, punch, thump. Assault, as in *a violence*. Should she list the catcalls from pickup truck windows? The naked feeling that comes when she stands at the corner in her skin-tight leggings, watching men in their cars out of the corner of her eye, trapped and waiting for the light to change? The unwanted brush of fingers along her low back in the bar? The hazy memory of muted resistance—to fingers, kisses—that weren't invited? Even those that were, that ended somewhere closer, more intimate, than she had ever intended. That she never knew how to resist except with silence first, then sound. Even sometimes, then, with love.

Later, she will learn to answer *yes* and *yes* and *yes* and *yes* and *yes* to all of these questions—at least, that is, in silence, to herself, to her memories. She will learn, in part, from talking to her mother. She will learn, in part, from talking to her friends. She will learn, in part, from reading and listening to the news about some very famous men, some very famous women, and one particularly famous lady lawyer whom her mother met once, many years ago. She will learn when her Facebook feed is overwhelmed, one evening, with a hashtag that makes her stomach curl and knuckles smart beyond the violence of her literal experience.

And that is when she will begin to wonder if there is something else. Something more echo than memory, more knowing than wound. A rape that, perhaps, she's inherited.

Should she call this knowing violence?

Medication Summary

All the vaccines. Calamine lotion to cover the spots that burnt her body when she got the chicken pox. SPF 45 or 55 or 70, if her mother had her way, all over her pink-pale skin, every summer. Lamisil for her nails when she was nineteen, to fix the yellow tinge that had taken hold (just as it did with her father). A drawer full of vitamins: B-Complex, C, E, and A.

Ortho Tri-Cyclen Lo for four years in her twenties, before she realized the pills were fucking with her hormones enough that she was contemplating getting pregnant on purpose to convince her boyfriend to stop smoking so much weed and get a job. Stashed probiotics and Advil gel tabs for long trips, bad cramps, the occasional hangover. Gardasil, the human papillomavirus (HPV) vaccine (too late) when she was twenty-seven. Before that, first cryotherapy and then a LEEP (loop electrosurgical excision procedure) to slice out all the blooming cells. "They look like cauliflower," the gynecologist had said.

All told, at least half a dozen boxes of Monistat 1. Nothing lately. She is grateful. She is holding her breath.

Medical History

On her mother's side: stroke, dementia, alcoholism, depression, PTSD, anxiety, high cholesterol, high blood pressure, Crohn's disease, and heart trouble. On her father's side: bad knees, melanoma, Parkinson's disease, diabetes, more high cholesterol, more high blood pressure. On the inside: mild anemia, low red-blood-cell count, low blood pressure, excellent cholesterol.

Later, she will add her own clinical anxiety and excessive alcohol consumption to this list. Later, there will be her own anxiety attacks and resultant low-dose prescription of Sertraline; her recognition of disordered drinking and realization that alcohol does not, in fact, engender intimacy or freedom; her apprehensive desire to disrupt these patterns and habits her body and consciousness seem to have relied upon since before they even began.

But she doesn't know that yet. For now, there is only that echo. That knowing. It takes the form of fear, a fear she can't explain and yet can't shake. Something about sex that feels invasive. Something about intimacy that feels like danger.

~~~

Later, when I am in my mid-thirties and the world is a different place, I will take a long walk on a sunny Idaho spring day. I will put my earbuds into my ears and turn on the *TED Radio Hour* podcast and listen to an episode on the biology of sex. Not sex as in the sex we have with people. Sex as in the sex we *are*, and how it happens. How, in fact, research now points to epigenetics as a pivotal determinant of gender identification relative to so-called sex, more accurately described as gonad assignment, and what this means for our future understanding of the critical relationship between epigenetics and gendered experience, between biological sex and brain chemistry. Later, I will continue to read about epigenetics and inherited trauma. About the growing evidence and confirmation that, indeed, pain and loss and hunger and violence and grief can bleed through generations—two, three, maybe more—on either or both sides, from mother or father, grandmothers and grandfathers. That entire schools of counseling and therapy have sprung up around the language we use to describe our struggles, our habits, our fears. That our genetic composition is a kind of
~~~

determinate layering of family narratives, of identifying elements, of words plucked and rearranged from the extant vocabulary of environment and influence present at our moment of becoming.

But I don't know that yet. All I know is what I've been told about my family and my body, what I've heard and felt and written down. All I know is that depressing story of my own conception—cheap booze, bad sex. That without them both, I would not exist at all.

Sex. Such a tiny, troubled word. Truncated container, only three letters long. Too small, I think, to bear the weight of bodies.

Then again, recall the fingers. The curve of the nails. So very small. So full of echoes.

Here are my fingers: pink with cold, crowned with nails just like my father's. Every now and then, I let my nails grow long, file tips to tidy almonds, then brush them over with some mauve or ox-blood polish. I like the way my painted fingers look in restaurant light: like jewels. Or against a lover's chest: the contrast. Something elegant and slick amid the flush of heated skin, raw scent. Damp sheets, then dry. The cotton stained with salt.

TWENTY-SEVEN

It is the summer of 2012. I am visiting my mother at her house in Chino, a house she purchased in the year following her separation from my father. Chino is a heavily agricultural town on the southeastern outskirts of Los Angeles, an aging suburb peppered with shabby swimming pools and luminous lemon trees. The area is known as the Inland Empire. Exquisitely hot.

Mom and I are in the kitchen: me at her new computer, Mom grazing near the sink. I'm helping her fill out a personal health history form so she can see a holistic nutritionist (my idea—I'm in the second of my twentysomething alternative health phases) about her chronic listlessness, perpetual indigestion, low moods, and crying jags. I'm living in a hippy enclave near the beach in San Diego and have recently begun working with this nutritionist, a perky Italian woman who gave a talk at my yoga studio. In other words, I'm proselytizing. It's a habit I picked up from my mother, one I've always resisted and should be able to recognize . . . but as annoying as I'm sure I am in this moment with my holier-than-thou attitude, Mom doesn't object. She's desperate for a solution.

"What is your current weight?" I ask, reading off the intake form.

"One sixty-five," she says, as she stands at the kitchen counter spooning tahini out of a squat metal jar and onto a rice cake. Her brown hair, still whorled from sleep, catches the light from the window over the sink, light that reveals whitish gray roots moving in under honey chestnut curls.

"And your weight six months ago?" I ask, punching the numbers into the fresh-out-of-the-box Apple keyboard.

"One sixty," she says, licking the rice cake from her lips.

"Ideal weight?"

"One thirty-five."

I scroll down and squint at the PDF file for the next set of questions. To counter my creeping smugness, I'm putting on my best secretarial tone—chirpy, brisk. "Okay. Now there's some personal background stuff."

"Fire away," Mom says. She is making a Bloody Mary.

"I went ahead and filled out the answers for 'Relationship Status' and 'Children' . . ."

She interjects, "Did you say that I'm divorced?"

"*Separated*, Mom." The chirpy voice evaporates in my mouth. "You're not divorced yet."

Mom pours about a quarter-cup of vodka into a pint glass, then adds V8, Worcestershire, lemon. No ice. She knows that I am right. As long as she and my father are still legally married, she gets to stay on his very excellent health insurance. Dad obliges—partly out of care, partly out of procrastinatory tendency. My mother, I suspect, is as relieved as she is resentful.

"Occupation?"

Mom pauses for a moment. "Homemaker." She hasn't received a paycheck since 1983, but no one can argue that she didn't manage our house, yard, bills, taxes, pets, and doctors' appointments like a pro throughout my childhood and teenage years. As if to punctuate her pronouncement, she takes a big bite of celery, then drops the rest of the spear into her drink with a flourish.

"Please list your main health concerns." I read the instructions aloud, my fingers poised and ready to punch in her answers, my mind already filling in the blanks.

"Lack of energy." It is eleven in the morning. I side-eye her Bloody Mary. But I also sympathize. She is lonely, bored, and practically allergic to the heat outdoors. The drink, a tiny shimmer in the otherwise relentless stretch of summer days.

"Let's see . . ." she continues. "Indigestion. Depression. Tired all the time. Apathy." She stops, takes another swig. "How old is this girl, do you think? The nutritionist? Is she really going to want to hear all this stuff about some old lady?" My mom always calls herself an "old lady," even though she is only sixty, and refers to every woman under the age of fifty-five as a "girl." The nutritionist is in her forties. I ignore the question.

"At what point in your life did you feel best?"

This is the next query on the form, and Mom's reply startles me with its quick assurance, its certainty.

"When I was twenty-seven," she says. "I felt my best when I was twenty-seven."

At this, I turn away from the screen to face her. She isn't looking at me, and I catch a moment within which to study her profile.

"What happened when you were twenty-seven?" I ask. I am twenty-seven. Twenty-seven and a half, to be precise.

"It was just before I started working at the Nurt," she says. The Nurt, short for the Nurtury, was a progressive preschool where my mom had been a teacher during her graduate studies in psychology. "I was in great shape; I felt pretty. I loved my job, and I had friends." Something about the simplicity of her answers gets stuck in my throat.

"Who were you dating back then?" I ask.

"Roger," she says, rolling her eyes. "The sock man."

It seems like all her ex-boyfriends have some distinguishing quirk, some oddity that bookmarks them in her memory. I don't have any ex-boyfriends—not really, anyway—and am still with the man who, to date, is my first and only serious partner, so I admittedly don't have much perspective. Later, I will understand that every woman has some version of my mother's nicknames, subtitles. I will collect my own. For her, there is the first Roger, a conscientious objector who asked her to elope to Canada during Vietnam; Steve, a carpenter with long red hair worn in a thick braid down to his butt who once got paid in Pringles chips for laying a parquet floor in Los Angeles; Andrew, the Morris dancer from England, with the motorcycle and the big nose; and the second Roger—this Roger of her twenty-seventh year—an intellectual effete who, according to my mother's stories and to her extreme distaste (she doesn't like anything that smacks of kink), had a thing for wearing socks during sex.

My mother has told me more than I should probably know for many years now—about these men, about my father, about other lovers and flings that came before and in between. I have intermittently hungered for and avoided her confidences, but rarely have I known when to end the conversation. By the time I was old enough to consider the benefit of boundaries around the details of my mother's sex life, it was too late to unhear them. Now I associate most epochs in her history with at least one of these men, often forgetting the single patches in between. Forgetting, or—at twenty-seven—not yet fully aware of just how much can happen within and between relationships. Relying on my own faulty memory and associative links to make sense of her story without recognizing when and where the gaps or inaccuracies—hers, mine—might be.

"We broke up that year, too, but it was fine. I was happy," she continues. "And it was . . . well, it was a wonderful time." She wrings the pint glass in her ringless left hand and looks out the window to the avocado trees in the yard.

"Of course, all that changed after the rape."

I am silent for a moment.

"What?"

She doesn't look at me. Instead, she drains her drink, then drops the heavy glass into the sink with a thud.

For several minutes, I wait. In the bright summer sunlight pouring in through the kitchen window, every second feels like an hour. Mom keeps gazing toward the avocado tree, heavy with fruit.

Finally, I get up from the desk and walk over to where she is standing against the kitchen counter. Just as I reach her, she begins to cry. I wrap my arms around her and rest my head on the crown of hers. She is five and a half feet tall. I am pushing six.

"I didn't know," I say. Even as the words come out, I second-guess. *Did* I know? Could I have known? "I'm so sorry."

She hugs me back, leaving a wet patch on my shoulder, then shuffles into the living room to lie down on the couch. The temperature is nearly a hundred degrees outside, but in here it is dark and cool. She keeps the air conditioner blasting and the blinds drawn, and while I usually find the atmosphere depressing, I am grateful for it now—the dim lights, the soft furniture.

Mom lies down on the blue couch with her head on a bright pink spangly pillow. Her eyes are red, like her nose, and there are dark wet smudges of last night's eyeliner pooling beneath her lower lashes. I sit at her feet, taking them one by one into my hands and massaging them like I used to do as a little girl when we'd watch TV, bargaining an extra massage in exchange for a later bedtime.

"He came up behind me while I was hanging laundry out back," she says at last, looking up again. "I had just come home from work. He grabbed my hair, held a knife to my neck." She lets out an incomprehensible little chuckle. "He said he wanted to be my boyfriend. But then, we found out later at the trial, he said the same thing to the seven other girls, too."

Even though it is the last thing in the world I want to do, I find myself imagining the scene: the faceless man, my mother, her long hair, the knife in his hands. As she speaks, I keep my gaze down, working her feet like worry dolls.

"His hair was like a curved broom," she continues. "I remember because it was so peculiar, not like anything else I had ever seen. Coarse and sleek at the same time." She shudders. "My dog Kahlua stayed under the bed, hiding, pissing herself."

There is a long silence. Mom's eyes stay closed, mine stay fixed on her feet.

"What happened to him?" I ask at last.

"Oh, I did the whole court thing," she says after a moment. "Testified, I mean. Me and one other girl, too." She sits up a little. "A lawyer called me, actually. A woman. She was gathering witnesses. She was young. We met up once or twice for dinner before the hearing."

I let out a small puff of air, a breath of relief. "So, he was convicted?"

She scoffs, "He got three years."

We don't talk about the rape story any more after that. Not that afternoon, and not for the following days of my visit. Instead, we drink wine and watch movies and swim in the pool and pick avocados and limes. For two days, I push it all down: push the story and the images and the worry down to the bottom of my consciousness.

On the third day, Mom drives me back home and drops me off at my apartment near the beach. The minute I walk through the door, I hear it all again: this memory, this story—hers, mine—blooming up inside my mind, between my ears.

I drown out the sound with domestic distractions. I unpack my clothes and open all of the windows, cook dinner and try to enjoy the smell of roasting vegetables—carrots, squash—and the warm wet scent of steaming brown rice. I feel like I should be afraid, but I am not. I cannot put a word to what I feel. It is partly sadness, of course, and partly sympathy. But it is also a hint of something that registers, perversely, like relief. A sensation of understanding, of diagnostic clarity. The cumulative effect of these feelings leaves me, when I try to face them, dazed.

If I am unsettled by the knowledge of my mother's trauma, I am also ashamed of my relative comfort, safety, protection, in this moment—in my apartment near the ocean with my boyfriend, a veteran who, I know, could protect me if I ever needed it. Of my gated apartment complex that is old, yes, but still with a keycode on the tall black metal fence outside and neighbors that I know and recognize. Of my second-story unit, and the window so high up. Of the fact that it is almost always my boyfriend who goes out back, beyond the gate, to do the laundry.

In the aftermath of this, my first hearing of my mother's story, it will not occur to me to link the anxiety attacks and shortness of breath that first led me back to yoga classes and thus to the holistic nutritionist in the first place with the information from my mother's health history intake form. With the stories of the men and the drinking and the rape. Instead, I will think primarily of the past: of my happy but sheltered, complicated childhood, my mother's fears, her many rules and clinging love. I will make the obvious connection: that my mother was hurt, traumatized, and therefore overprotective of her daughter. I will have the superficial realization: that what I think I know about my mother's life might not be wholly accurate.

INTERLUDE: BACKGROUND MUSIC

1990

Corners of another four o'clock. Curl in upon this: kitchen, window, tile, sink. Yellow unlike zinnias or butter, something by Mozart on the radio.[1] *You are five, or six, and painting watercolors on the kitchen floor: paintbrush dipped in Star Trek coffee mugs of water in between each shade of yellow, purple, pink. Spock, or maybe Sulu; someone broke the Captain Kirk cup during that pocket of time in which you lived but did not yet know how to remember.*[2] *Ten years prior to all this: the vintners at Sutter Home invented mom's white Zinfandel by accident. In 1975, 1,000 grape-squeezed gallons stalled en route to fermentation, holding*

---

[1] You are sure of this: the certainty that you cannot be certain. Memory is not a transcript. What's most akin to fact is four o'clock: it's sickly gorgeous bright. What makes this true is that this brightness happens every day (or nearly), and the light makes something in your blood and nerves begin to hum.

[2] You do *not* want to call your mother. You do not want the telephone, or the sound of the Volvo in the drive, or dinner smells. You want to be outside, alone, and moving through it—light, that is, and time.

sugar, fighting dryness, blushing pink and sweet and easier to swallow.[3] *Above you, all around you, she is barefoot: as she boils water, dumps a jar of Newman's Own spaghetti sauce into the pot, adds chunks of garlic, carrot, and tomato; as the wall phone rings and clicks, and as you hear the cork pop in your fingers, feel the sound against your teeth.*[4] *And because all of this, too, occurs in that stalled pocket of time—that is, the time in which you lived and painted watercolors and smelled Newman's Own spaghetti sauce and garlic, and heard Mozart on the radio, and felt the brown and cream faux marble tile underneath your skinny-kid legs, and saw your mother's clean bare feet and never-painted toe nails, and heard them stick and unstick on the tile as she moved from phone to stove to bottle—you cannot say you remember dinnertime was five or six or seven*[5]*—hearing the blue automatic Volvo in the driveway, running to the door before darkness came. How corks accumulated in the junk drawer*[6] *and the curl of autumn. How the light at four o'clock still makes your molars sing, then itch.*

---

[3] You want to move toward the dark. Not to make it happen faster, necessarily; just to get beyond the curl.

[4] Just to use the light, to trace its shape against the leaves and sidewalk shadows.

[5] Resist the urge to scratch your teeth. To notice how the reddish light of four o'clock does something to your skin.

[6] An inverse power structure here: as long as you are not inside, its curling cannot take you.

WOMAN HOUSE

I grew up watching old movies with my mother. Together, we'd sit side by side, our bodies parallel, sunk within the plush and fold of oversized living-room armchairs—one champagne cream, one cabernet red—each with a wineglass filled to the brim (mine with apple juice and sparkling water, hers with something pink or white poured from an economy-size bottle) balanced on the table between us.

After school, I'd flip through the Turner Classic Movies TV guide and circle titles I wanted to see, skim for the names of actors I loved, that I'd learned to love because my mother loved them first: Jimmy Stewart, Olivia de Havilland, Tyrone Power. We watched Errol Flynn and de Havilland period pieces. Humphrey Bogart and Lauren Bacall noir films. Fred Astaire and Ginger Rogers song-and-dance romances. Cary Grant and Katherine Hepburn comedies. Of this last category, one of our most beloved and most frequently viewed was *The Philadelphia Story*.

I probably saw *The Philadelphia Story* for the first time when I was eleven, maybe twelve. I remember being introduced to this film as a classic, a story of sophisticated humor and social commentary, a multiple Academy Award winner. I can recall my child body, how sometimes I would balance my imaginary wine against my fingers like a cocktail glass, how sometimes I would borrow my mother's matte black pumps and pace back and forth across the kitchen linoleum, drink in hand, listening to the satisfying, rhythmic click of my heels during the opening credits.

Decades later, I am finally rewatching, reconsidering, with closer attention.

~~~

My senior year of college, I shared a dormitory apartment with three women. Suite I: our collective address, our collective nickname. Of the four of us, I was the only virgin. At my age, among my friends and peers, this made me an anomaly.

I'd spent my junior year abroad living in Dublin, Ireland. I'd never lived alone before, or in a city. I was not yet twenty-one when I arrived in Dublin and felt lawless ordering beer at the bar. But order I did, and I spent my days drinking Guinness while reading Heaney and Boland and Joyce, learning how to walk fast alone on city streets, mix a gin and tonic, boil rice, dye my own hair. It was a time of unprecedented freedom for me, my first-ever opportunity to experiment with truly unfettered time and expectations. At twenty, however, I struggled to appreciate this liberty as much as I would later, in retrospect, come to value and miss it. If I was free, I was also acutely lonely. Imbued in every city ramble, every solitary sit at a café or pub, was the flickering hope for something—someone—to happen. I yearned for a grand European adventure to somehow change my life.

By "European adventure," I mean relationship. I hoped that I would meet someone in Dublin and fall in love like they did in the movies and books I'd devoured as a child.

It is worth noting that this was 2005. That I had taken only one
~~~

sociology class and was as yet unversed in anything even remotely close to contemporary feminism. That my mother, despite living out her twenties in the hedonistic, progressive spaces of the LA art scene of the 1970s, was not herself a practicing feminist—had not even been aware of, let alone visited, Judy Chicago and Miriam Schapiro's 1972 *Womanhouse* feminist art installation located in a ramshackle mansion on Hollywood's Mariposa Avenue, just a few short miles from where Mom and her boyfriend had lived in Echo Park. That she had not raised me with any critical awareness of the values and ideas behind what she still, to this day, refers to as "the women's movement." It is worth providing some context. What little I understood about the patriarchy and female liberation I had gleaned, not surprisingly, from plots of novels like *Little Women* and *Jane Eyre* and *Northanger Abbey*, and from the machinations of European history . . . but this awareness was hardly integrated into my social life, let alone intersectional in scope. I was—blissfully, painfully—ignorant of the patriarchal influence churning beneath the surface of my hunger for amorous male attention. I knew only that I wanted it. And that drinking made it easier to get.

Perhaps, then, it is also not surprising that what happened in Dublin and several other European cities thereafter wasn't so much romance as a series of underwhelming, sloppy trysts with fellow exchange students. The darkened kitchen fumblings of a Dartmouth student, his mouth wet on mine after too many beers, his fingers abruptly grappling with the slight hook of my clearance-priced, dark blue Calvin Klein bra; the scent of spiced beans and savory pastry mingled with pot smoke and the sticky-noxious sweetness of spilled liquor surrounding my body as I allowed it to fall—briefly—into bed with a very stoned Brazilian at his sister's party hours after we'd met on a bridge at midnight on New Year's Eve in Paris. With them, these strange men, I'd felt excited and reckless at first, then afraid. Sharply aware, despite the alcoholic fog involved in each instance, that these interactions were intimate in action only. That I had let the drinking push me past the point of choice and into something darker. It was only when I was alone again, back on the Dublin streets, that I felt a growing ease in my own body. An ease dependent on my solitude and solitary motion, walking in the city. Blazer pockets for my hands. Flat shoes. Steady speed.

And yet that ease came at the cost of companionship. Repeatedly, I yearned for something to propel me back into the arms of another. I did not know, or perhaps was too afraid to learn, how to seek connection earnestly, in the light of day. If there was danger lurking in that foggy darkness, there was also a different kind of freedom—from accountability, from clarity of purpose, from the responsibility to choose.

By the time I returned to my Vermont campus in the fall of 2006, that Dublin year had settled beneath my skin: the walk, a habit; the hair dye, a regular routine; the drinking, a moderate but consistent source of solace and, at times, sought-after oblivion—a catalyst to propel me into circumstances where the possibility of intimacy felt heightened, to push me past my fears in the hope that something better lay beyond; the unspent yearning, a ball of shame I did my best to shove out of sight.

~~~

"The thing that's interesting to people is whether the woman is happy in this house or whether she is trying to hide." So writes Louise Bourgeois of a specific line drawing in ink from her mid-century *Femme maison* series, this one dated 1947.

The figure in each *Femme maison*—French for "housewife" or, translated literally, "woman house"—has a different energy and mood to her body, structure, predicament. Some are in color, while others are black and white. Two appear to have smoking chimneys or perhaps are on fire. One is jumping into the air; another waves; still another towers, armless, her upper body and head elongated into a leaning skyscraper (or a cucumber, or a phallus). But it is my favorite *femme* which Bourgeois describes in the quote above,
~~~

taken from her book of drawings and observations, and published under the same title.

What I notice as I look at this drawing—and I look often—is the flatness with which the woman's body is outlined versus the depth conveyed by simple lines and shading in the windows of the house, the wooden floorboards upon which the woman stands, her feet neatly arranged in an almost-balletic first position. I notice the disproportionately small hand waving from the upper story of her house-head—its tiny, childish fingers—and the contrast with her other, longer arm hanging by her side. I notice and appreciate the simple hip curve and the swoop of a line Bourgeois situates below the waist to indicate a stomach, a bit of a pooch. Upon the knees, similar swoops.

This woman is a real woman with a real body, a body like my own, with age and sag and belly and the hint of pubic hair delineated in two quick lines to the left of the relaxed triangle suggesting her genitalia. And yet she, the woman-house inside this body-building, is denied all properties of depth. Only the house itself, its arched windows, and the ground (manmade) upon which the woman stands denote perspective.

I love this drawing because it feels relatable in ways I struggle to admit to myself but can see and feel so clearly in Bourgeois's deceptively simple rendering: the selfhood, the authenticity of this woman squashed into a single dimension beneath the viewer's gaze.

~~~

The Philadelphia Story was released in 1940. Directed by George Cukor and based on the 1939 play of the same name, it stars Katherine Hepburn as Tracy Lord, a socialite living at home with her mother and sister after the failure of her first marriage to alcoholic yacht designer C. K. Dexter Haven (Carey Grant), which ended with her kicking him out for his moral failings. Tracy won't put up with Dexter's drinking or, more recently, her father's affair, and as
~~~

the movie opens, she is encouraging her mother to stand up for herself and likewise dissolve her own marriage as a matter of principle. Tracy herself is poised to remarry, this time to a wealthy and upstanding new-money businessman named George. Then Dexter shows up—sober, but with a mischievous glint in his eye—together with a pair of tabloid reporters eager to cover the impending society wedding, and a blackmail scheme designed to ingratiate them into the Lord household.

What ensues is billed as "a comedy of remarriage," a category trendy in the 1930s and 1940s—films filled with sexual innuendo and pseudo-extramarital affairs that could fly under the radar of the conservative Hays Code because they were cloaked as screwball comedies. Growing up, I loved *The Philadelphia Story* (and, for that matter, many of the other films in this subgenre—*The Awful Truth*, *Bringing Up Baby*, *My Favorite Wife*). Now, however, I feel a growing discomfort with scenes and suggestions that I once saw as amusing and light.

Consider, for instance, the prologue: Hepburn's Tracy is unceremoniously pushed to the ground by Grant's Dexter after she breaks one of his golf clubs across her thigh. Tracy throws the broken club at Dexter's feet, her white nightgown buttoned tightly at her neck, her regal nose in the air. In response, Dexter makes as if to strike, then instead presses his palm squarely into her face. Grant's palm is soft. The blow and resultant fall defy physics. Both, as the whimsical soundtrack reassure us, are being played for laughs. A little light domestic abuse to get things going. Tracy rubs her neck with a grimace. The iconic theme music swells.

When I was young, I mostly paid attention to the comic pratfall and the exaggerated faces in this scene. Watching it again now, I'm horrified. Even more so to realize how this introduction anticipates the narrative arc: that Tracy is falsely idolized for her great beauty coupled with her high moral standards and will ultimately fall from grace—not only fall but then thank the men who have toppled her from her pedestal. As the film progresses, hole after hole is poked into Tracy's surface veneer of desirability. We are told that virtue (as in, sexual virtue) isn't truly attractive to men, or even truly good; that passing judgment on the foibles of others (mainly drunkenness and promiscuity) is neither womanly nor wifely nor daughterly behavior; that keeping up appearances to avoid public exposure or gossip is neither admirable nor worth the compromise to one's authenticity.

What that authenticity is, of course, and whether it is feasible for anyone in Tracy's position—indeed, for any woman who is caught within the machinations of society life, of patriarchy—is another question all together.

~~~

By October of my senior year in college, I'd begun to get my own taste of public exposure. Friends would confide that they'd been asked about me—the tall girl with the broad shoulders and the red hair. *Who was she? Where had she come from?* Many of these questions, it seemed, began in the minds and mouths of men I remembered from previous semesters. Men to whom, during those first two years on campus, I had apparently been invisible. Men who now watched me as I walked. I imagined, at the time, that I had somehow brought back with me a kind of mystique. That my red dyed hair and the jeans I'd bought in Barcelona bestowed upon me what my roommate called "the X factor"—that undefinable something that made an otherwise average-looking woman magnetic to the men in her midst.

Mine was a small college, so perhaps these minor differences in my appearance really were enough to set me apart. But what I didn't realize until late in the semester was that there was also a rumor: one that had begun in my own home, from my roommate's mouth, a rumor that had spiraled out to a cohort of men one evening at their off-campus house. My roommate had told her new boyfriend and his gathered friends that I was still a virgin. From that moment
~~~

on, their collective pursuit of me became a game. The men jockeyed for position: who would get to try first?

I didn't find out about this for months. All I knew was that, for the first time I could recall, I found myself desired—not just in a moment of intimacy, but socially, publicly. It was a heady experience. The awareness of so much collective desire directed at me—that is, at my body, and at a time when I hadn't yet realized that desire for my body and desire for myself weren't mutually exclusive—was utterly new.

I had no reason, then, to fear the men who watched me in Vermont the way I'd feared the men in Dublin. I had not yet developed the conscious awareness that to be seen like this—from a distance, as a vessel for the desires of others, my body a predetermined narrative—was in and of itself a kind of flattening. Was its own kind of violence.

~~~

The woman who resides within a house might be powerful or she might be trapped. She might be content or strategizing an escape. More likely, many of these things are true for the woman. They overlap—with one another, with her experience of being in a body.

In her 2005 interpretation of that specific *Femme maison* illustration from 1947, American art historian Mignon Nixon posits that "something is happening inside, upstairs, where she lives. The woman is thinking, talking, working, or perhaps she dreams."

Of this same drawing, Bourgeois continues, "Well obviously, it is a woman who hides."

I like—no, I relate to—this conflation, this overlap: of course, a woman who is hiding is also active, thinking. Of course, she is both. Why else would she think to hide? She might be hiding on purpose, biding her time, or she might be voluntarily oblivious, imagining away the realities surrounding her. Then again, none of the *femmes* appear particularly placid. Even those who are armless,
~~~

motionless, suggest, in their stillness, a quiet desperation. Maybe not so quiet, in fact, if the pluming hair or smoke or flame escaping from the roofs of their houses is any indication of what's going on upstairs. And Bourgeois's work is nothing if not a celebration and exploration of the contradictory: something playful here, something grotesque there. Innocence and sexuality. Freedom and constraint. The rotund, organic female body and the geometric shapes of the manmade world.

Bourgeois's *Femme maison*, Nixon contends, at once refuses, subverts, and mocks her counterparts rendered at the hands of male surrealist artists like Andre Masson and Marcel Jean, whose *Mannequin* works—idealized, slender female figures with birdcage heads, mascaraed lashes, pansy-stuffed mouths—featured prominently at the 1938 International Exhibition of Surrealism in Paris. The *Femme maison*, Nixon insists, is "neither medusa nor madonna, muse nor mannequin . . . but a new feminine type, a figure struggling to free herself from the burdens of displacement and domesticity, motherhood and masculine desire."

Though her head may be trapped in house after house, her body resists: sometimes with arms reaching, flying, her legs spread, her hair billowing from the rooftop, wild like fire.

"In Masson's *Mannequin*, what is sexual . . . is not exposed, but covered," Nixon continues. If the surrealist men sought to silence women, to fetishize their concealed sexuality, to make their bodies into statues, Bourgeois makes the sex of her *Femmes maisons* irrepressible, cartoonish, and loud. There is a boisterousness to these bodies: an ungainly noise to their saggy knees, truncated breasts, lumpy hips, shameless genitals. They are a little weird—or, seen another way, they are refreshingly realistic.

Overtly physical, their eyeless bodies wink at us even as they may squirm, stuck as they are. They ask us to examine our own assumptions of privacy, of agency.

~~~
~~~

My mom had many rules about TV and movies when I was growing up. She disapproved of most contemporary sitcoms, for instance, as well as music videos and true-crime shows. Anything with overt references to violence, sex, or drugs. I was—am—an only child, perpetually sheltered. I'm sure my mother thought she was protecting me with these rules. She didn't let me watch *Friends*, for instance, even though all the girls at school watched it. She didn't like the promiscuity of *Friends*, the fact that so much of the basic plot revolved around sex and dating or dating and sex within a group of young, underemployed twentysomethings.

But when it came to markers of so-called culture and class, I suspect both my parents were—are—susceptible to smoke and mirrors and that, by extension, so was I. After all, those movies from the 1930s and 1940s with their Oscar wins and iconic stars, so elegant in black and white, the men always dressed in suits, the women buttoned up in lipstick and tweed, all the drinks in pretty crystal glasses, all the sex invisible and off screen, offered up an obscured portrait of reality: of perpetual misogyny, violence, sexism, racism, casual alcohol abuse, and the objectification of women taking place in plain sight.

When it came to the overlap of cinema and sex, my rules growing up revolved around concealment. History, literature, and culture were fine. Alcohol and cigarettes were fine, too. And the sex, or the allusion thereto, was fine if it was subtle. That is, as long as the sex didn't show. As long as you couldn't smell it.

Although the society home at the center of *The Philadelphia Story* is perpetually glossed with such subterfuge, Tracy's little sister Dinah is the only one interested in puncturing her family's façade of perfection. She is probably eleven, maybe twelve. She excels in the art of the micro-rebellion. She eavesdrops. She mispronounces words (my favorite, *innundo* for *innuendo*—"It was full of innundo!" she tells her mother, after reading the tabloid reports about her sister's first failed marriage and subsequent divorce). She strides around the house in trousers, expertly working a yo-yo and shouting at the top of her voice. She says "stinks" instead of "stinking," and is equally willing to frankly acknowledge the opposite: when complimented on her dress for Tracy's wedding, she does not say thank you. Instead, she nods and adds, "I smell good, too!"

Dinah courts danger, scandal, absurdity, freedom. She is just young enough to perhaps be free of that hyper-gendered awareness of herself and her body that will inevitably set in as she becomes a teenager. Because, of course, Dinah was raised inside the house, the high society around which the film's tabloid charade revolves. Rebellious as she may appear on screen, she is also being groomed, no doubt, to take Tracy's place as the eligible society daughter, the future wife and mother. Sooner or later, the suffocating cloche of social expectation will slip down over her head, her neck, her chest.

Watching her mischievous eyes snooping at the window, her hands flying across the piano keys, I can't help but think of Dinah as a peer to Bourgeois and her *femmes maisons*. Try as she might, even her rebellions come with borders: with the bounds of the walls and floorboards that give her dimension, that contextualize the existence of her body in space. And I begin to see in her a version of myself, the self who likewise learned about relationships and sex and expectations from a character like Tracy.

~~~

I look back at a photograph of myself at twenty-two, sitting in the common room of our dorm. I see the image of my younger body, tucked inside this women's house. This self: curled to one side, her legs angled out of frame. Left ankle and a flash of bare heel visible above the lip of a moccasin slipper. Her mouth, tight; a turning down beneath the point of nose and heavy eyes. She looks tired, though perhaps that is in part a trick of eyeliner and shadow. Or perhaps she has been drinking. Her hair is a chaos: sideswept purple-auburn bangs and loose strands strewn across her left brow and over her ear, the curve of messy bun a darkness. I can see the
~~~

left back pocket of her jeans, the way her body twists. Her left arm is wrapped across her waist, the weight of it held not so much to flatten, it would seem, as to protect. To conceal.

I don't recall who took the photograph, or when. What I do know is what was happening around her—around me, this version of myself from fifteen years ago, a self I recognize but struggle to identify or feel within my body now, at thirty-six, save for that impulse to hold myself close.

What I know, or at least remember, is this: the heady feeling waned. The desire I had so enjoyed at first, the sensation of desire directed at my body, the heat of collective eyes along the skin of my neck, began to scorch.

That is, until I met a man I liked more than I wanted to admit, and my defenses faltered. He had chlorine-bleached hair and faded blue Vans and a Ken Kesey novel in his back pocket. When I realized that I did, in fact, want to kiss and touch this man, I was frightened—not of the prospect of sex per se, but of the prospect of desired intimacy and the threat of rejection. It was not an empty insecurity. Early in our affair, the two of us barely clothed and lying together in his bed, he told me that he was worried, too, albeit for different reasons: he did not want the burden of sleeping with me—the responsibility of what it would mean, he said, to "take" my virginity.

This was bad enough. Embarrassing, since it clearly indicated his lack of interest in a real relationship with me—the kind of relationship I was sure, in my infatuation, I desired from him. Even worse, he was my roommate's boyfriend's roommate. There was no hiding this, my habit of following him home from the bar at night, his habit of asking me to stay (but not to be his girlfriend). No concealing my willingness to compromise what I wanted for his sustained attention. Waking up in his bed meant encountering my roommate in the bathroom or in the kitchen moments after—getting water, brushing teeth, playing with the tiny orange kitten, Mona, and her razor claws. Letting little Mona scratch and gnaw my skin like she did my roommate's so I could prove that I, too, belonged in that house. Letting the man's cigarette smoke cling to my hair so I could smell it in the shower, let his presence follow me home.

But back at Suite I, my roommate kept warning me against the Kesey-reading, Vans-wearing surfer. She confirmed what I suspected: that he wasn't interested in anything serious. I didn't want to believe her, so I said it wasn't any of her business. We argued. I felt manipulated, the way she spoke of me to her boyfriend and his roommate when I wasn't there, the way they had collectively, it seemed, decided that I could and would only sleep with a man who wanted to be my boyfriend. That I was too much of a "good girl" for anything else. I struggled to see my roommate's protective instincts for what they were, probably because I knew that her warnings were true. Besides, I was angry. Not just angry. I felt flattened by this—the dynamic, the close quarters of my entwined friendships, courtships.

If only I could make my body less precious, I reasoned. Rid myself of this burden, the supposed value that seemed to rob me of power and permit others to patronize me even as they put my body onto a pedestal.

By spring, I wasn't preserving my virginity for moral reasons. Or maybe I was, but that wasn't the language or rationale to which I consciously adhered. Sunday-school lessons and maternal warnings aside, I did not believe there was anything sinful or bad about sex before marriage, even sex before love. Part of me wanted more than anything to be like my peers, like the liberated women of 1990s and early 2000s television, like the imagined singletons on *Friends* (a series I had finally watched, in its entirety, during that Dublin year spent living alone). Not "sleeping around," per se, but easygoing about sex and sexuality, about my body interacting with other bodies. But deep down, I was also waiting for a sense of rightness. How could I not? My subliminal sex-ed, courtesy of the Hays Code, had taught me to hold out in the face of unwanted advances and seductive lust, to stay true past the point of reason or let myself be caught unawares by a sudden, charming, providential stranger. Either narrative, a romance. Either way, a love story.

Increasingly, at least to my conscious, intellectual mind, rightness aligned less with romance or affection or commitment than it did with efficacy. How to neutralize this open secret. How to de-fetishize my body, reclaim some sense of dimension beyond the token identity I'd taken on as the virgin to be claimed (or avoided). How to climb down from that pedestal—that cage—of others' desire and simply move in the world, freely and without constraint.

~~~

"It has to do with the fact that this woman, who is hiding, is not conscious," Bourgeois continues in her description of *Femme maison, 1947*. "And consciousness and unconsciousness, as I said before, interest me today. A lot of the things we do, we do because we are in a state of high or because we are in a state of repression or because we are in a state that is not our usual state."

I think about Bourgeois's take on her unconscious woman house as I rewatch the pivotal wedding-eve scenes from *The Philadelphia Story* and can't help but see the parallels in Tracy's story—hers, and mine. How Dexter accuses Tracy of aspiring to be a "goddess," some sort of citadel of purity "to be taken" by the right man. How George promises, then, to "worship" her (poor timing, George), only moments before her father then accuses her of being a statue of a woman, incapable of the "foolish, unquestioning, uncritical affection" that helps men remain loyal to their partners.

Whether or not these criticisms of Tracy and Tracy's own criticisms of others are well founded—when this scene takes place, she is chastising her mother for returning to her father despite his very public affair—is beside the point. It is better, we are to understand, for a woman to be foolish than it is for her to be correct, to be justified in her anger, her opinions.
~~~

Sure, I think, as I rewatch these scenes: Tracy, in her patronizing, judgmental mode is unappealing. Her social snobbery is obnoxious, classist, and unattractive. But is it fair to lump her censure of her father, of her ex-husband—their respective betrayals, the pain of their prioritizations (of lust, of alcohol)—in with the social mores Tracy was forced to learn by these very men, by the society they forged around her?

"What's the matter with everyone all at once, anyhow?" Tracy mumbles. She walks inside to find a tray filled with tiny elegant coupes of champagne. Examines the glasses. Downs one, then two, then three.

What follows is a series of booze-fueled amorous and comic antics intended to demonstrate *in vino veritas*—and, as such, a glimpse of "the real Tracy." I did not know it as a child, watching this film, but now I can say, with deep certainty and a throb of shame, that even the truest of drunken confessions are only half the story—are always, inevitably, muddled in contradiction and false agency. Something else is always hiding underneath. Something is always being concealed, protected, whether the drinker—speaker—is aware of it or not.

And so I watch Hepburn as she upturns each coupe, her hair—famously red, even if it isn't visible in black and white—somehow glowing, lit up in its signature cascade across her shoulders. I watch her and I wince with empathy as she continues, the look on her face one of neither enjoyment nor abandon, but determination. To force a change in her body, her psyche, her circumstances. To blunt the sharp edges of her resistance and her mind.

~~~

The truth is, the advent of my drinking put everything into motion. Proximity to men, proximity to sex. Perhaps I always knew it would, soaked through as my consciousness had always been with the glamour and ubiquity of alcohol buzzing in the background (and
~~~

the foreground) of my family's life. My mom drank daily: cooking dinner, watching movies, talking on the phone. Pretty much any time after 3 or 4 or 5 p.m. was drinking time. My dad would drink a few beers after work, wine at restaurants or on special occasions. Meanwhile, all the characters in the black and white films went dancing at nightclubs, hosted cocktail parties, then came home to elegant apartments and decanters of whiskey.

If my parents didn't encourage or permit me to drink in my teen years, they also didn't hide or actively discourage the practice, nor did they make any effort to temper the idea that alcohol was at once sophisticated and perfectly acceptable as an everyday indulgence, a softener to slow things down at the end of the day.

When I finally decided to try beer at a college party, it didn't feel scary. The choice, the act, felt like rites of passage, behaviors I'd been anticipating, biding my time to adopt into my life. Exciting, sure: the yeast-sweet of Miller High Life, the bubbles on my tongue, the starry feeling behind my temples. But not forbidden. What felt forbidden was the change that came when I started drinking around men. This was a different atmosphere all together: a loosening of something in my body, some protective instinct. A willingness to test myself against the unknowns of other bodies. If I had subconsciously expected that this would be the case, it was another thing entirely to experience it firsthand, at a party, around strangers. To let this artificial shift in consciousness dull the sharp delineation of my fears, the precision of my romantic ideals, into something malleable. Accessible. Fluid.

The night I finally had sex for the first time, it was not with the man I wanted, the man who was my roommate's boyfriend's roommate. It was with another man instead, one who had been flirting with me and following me around for several weeks in a quiet, unthreatening kind of way. He was attractive and popular, and—a silly but relevant detail—shorter than me. If I had to give a reason for why I picked him, it would be that he seemed simultaneously like a catch (he played guitar in a popular campus band), and like a safe bet. I can remember thinking that, when the word got out, I would not be embarrassed. I remember very little of the sex itself. This is not because I was drunk, though I had indeed been drinking. I drank the necessary amount to make sure I would go through with my plan, but not enough to be sloppy.

Perhaps memory fails because the sex was unremarkable. (It was.) Or perhaps because I was ashamed. (I was.) Or perhaps because I didn't want this sex, the mechanics alone significant in my memory, to really *count*. Or perhaps because the circumstances surrounding my decision to sleep with this other man enacted an emotional trauma upon me, a form of self-harm I couldn't recognize until many, many years later.

Here is what I do remember: pockets of space and image around the encounter itself, before and after. There had been a party. It was a big party, in a much-coveted dormitory apartment with a spiral staircase. I had hoped to see the man I wanted at the party. When, after several hours, I did not, I left with this other man instead. It had, I think, been something of a test: a subconscious wager with the men, and with myself. I couldn't tell you, in the end, who won.

~~~

I admire Nixon's insistent reclamation of the figure in *Femme maison, 1947*, as a rebel against patriarchal structures and fetishized female sexuality. In many ways, I believe her ideas hold up even when put into conversation with Bourgeois's own observations on the drawing. There is a definitive both-and principle at work in this simultaneously cartoonish, sweet, subversive, and playful body on the page. "Unlike the rigid poses of the woman as fetish," Nixon notes, in describing the woman's waving hand reaching upward from the windows of the house, "these are the active gestures of the subject who lives in and through her body . . . in relation to others."

That relationship, however, complicates the rebellious reading of the body. Exposure alone, overt sex alone, does not agency make.
~~~

The woman's active gestures, her waving and moving and thinking and trying, all come at a cost. After all, to whom does she wave? From whom does she attempt to hide? How is she already trapped in the context of her existence, situated, as she is, just off center on the strictly lined, squarely wooden floor?

"This woman is obviously nice looking," says Bourgeois, "but she does not realize the effect she has on us. She does not know that she is half naked, and she does not know that she is trying to hide. That is to say, she is totally self-defeating because she shows herself at the very moment she thinks she's hiding."

What I see in the *Femme maison* is not unlike what I see in Tracy's drunken rebellion: her active gestures, her mirthful wave, suggest a limited—and, as such, deeply poignant—agency. She is just conscious enough to hide, or attempt to hide, with intention, but not conscious enough to fully recognize the trap that has been set beneath and around her body. She believes she is being honest, vulnerable, in her state of semi-undress, but she doesn't see that neither true authenticity nor a return to privacy are possible for her. She cannot remove the house, or see where to place her feet, or recognize to whom she waves, what kind of attention she is seeking.

~~~

Back at my dorm: I can picture the used condom and its wrapper in the trash. The pilled bright blue of my cheap bedsheets. My naked body, bare feet on the common room linoleum. The thrifted kimono robe—worn silk, pink and gold with cascading flowers and black trim—that I wrapped around myself after the man left Suite I in the morning.

And I can remember feeling a change. Not one of maturity, or womanhood, or violence. Certainly not the imprint of romance, or even of desire. I can't remember if I ever really felt desire for this man, whom I slept with several more times after that first, so much as I felt a reaction in my body to *his* desire for *me*, a reaction
~~~

sweetened by the inevitable alcohol that saturated those final weeks before graduation, drifting earlier and earlier into the day in the form of mimosa brunches under wide white tents, or gin and tonics with visiting relatives on the endless expanse of blue-green lawn. There was a liquored haze in the air once final exams and thesis deadlines passed and all of us, it seemed, were spending our days in celebration beneath the heavy clouds and humid breezes of late May in central Vermont.

If anything, I would call my brief relationship with this man, our nights together, a mutual exchange: each of us got what we were seeking from one another. He had wanted to sleep with me, and he did. I never quite understood his reasoning, but since he was kind and gentle and neither gossiped about me nor pressured me for a more serious relationship, I was content not to know. Meanwhile, I had wanted to choose with whom I lost my virginity, to "make it happen" under circumstances I deemed at once physically safe, emotionally safe, and socially acceptable, and I did. As far as I was concerned, we'd broken even.

This is what disturbs me about these decisions now, though: the entire relationship, and the change I felt as a result, was one of precision. Of calculus. A cold removal from the intimacy involved. A scalpel removing the offending article (virginity) and the enlistment or manipulation of a man to help me achieve my ends. At the time, I thought I'd conducted a fair risk-benefit analysis. That I'd weighed the likelihood of hurting this man and found it minimal. That my strategy, if not quite a secret, had at least been a success. It never occurred to me to include my own potential harm in the equation.

~~~

The night before her wedding, Tracy drinks herself into a champagne-fuzzed oblivion. She dances with the charming, likewise boozed-up Mike, the handsome tabloid reporter played by Jimmy Stewart, and ends up kissing him in the early hours of the morning.
~~~

The pair then decides to swim—that is, until Tracy hits the water and, in Mike's words, "the wine hits her." He carries her to her bedroom, her bare feet wiggling in drunken glee, her body wrapped in a robe. Though nothing untoward happens beyond that initial kiss, Mike leaves his watch in Tracy's bedroom, and that damning error—together with Dinah's peeping perspicacity—sets the stage for the closing comedy of hungover confusion in which Tracy is led to believe she slept with Mike, that her virtue and self-righteousness have alike been compromised, that she no longer has any right to judge or criticize anyone for drunkenness or infidelity.

All of this, of course, leads to Tracy's revelation that she does not love George and is in fact still in love with Dexter. That she needed a night of human error to remember the fullness of herself, her desires, and to recognize the power of forgiveness in the face of everyone else's human errors, too.

Forgiveness is, I think, an act of genuine consciousness. A clarity of mind and heart that allows one to see humanity in oneself and others, to care for both with equal generosity. What bothers me about the ending of *The Philadelphia Story* isn't this forgiveness narrative. It's the alcohol-driven catalyst that gets us there. As an adult, I no longer know what to make of Dexter, whose sobriety plays a subtle but essential role in the plot of the film and allows him to turn the tables on Tracy while maintaining empathy for her physical and emotional hangover on the morning of her wedding, using Tracy's belief in her own ruin and her fear of having to face the gathered crowd of guests with no groom at her side to convince her—swiftly, in a matter of seconds—to remarry him instead. I'm not sure how to reconcile Dinah, delighted, taking credit for engineering the match with her peeping and "innundo" and unabashed loyalty to Dexter. I'm disappointed at Tracy's abrupt declaration of defeat—"I'm such an unholy mess of a girl"—and valorization of Dexter as the one who "tried to stand her on her feet" in the aftermath of all her failings. I'm frustrated by the speed with which screwball comedy conventions of 1940s cinema necessarily bulldoze through the layered, nuanced, painful reality of these complex relationships in the interest of a "happy" (read: married) ending.

But most of all, I am bothered by the notion that drinking oneself into a state of false consciousness can and will result not only in a revelation of authentic selfhood and desire, but also in the finding and securing of true love. That for someone unaccustomed to such indulgence, like Tracy, one good bender might be all it takes to unlock lifelong happiness.

~~~

On the night before graduation, I wore my dyed red hair long and loose. On my feet, suede leather moccasins, easily slipped off so I could feel the dewy blue-green grass between my toes. I drank with abandon that night, all night. I drank enough to lift and float my body through the space and dark, to move my lips against the lips of others—lovers, friends—whom I hoped I'd miss, or whom I hoped might someday miss me. It was a blurry distinction, and the alcohol only made it blurrier, which helped. In a sugared fog, I didn't have to decide.

Eyes ringed with mascara, feet stained with dirt, I barely had time to change into a dress and brush my teeth the next morning, to smear concealer under my eyes and across my shiny nose. It was a wet day, with gray-damp clouds. I remember waiting in a line, grateful for the intermittent rain and greasy breakfast sandwiches someone handed out to us, for the cool water on my skin and the salt enlivening my still-drunk tongue. I remember sweating in between the bouts of breeze and rain, the polyester blue of my graduation gown hugging the Vermont humidity to my neck and the bottoms of my thighs. I remember walking on the damp grass when my turn came; hearing *phi beta kappa* and *summa cum laude* as I crossed the wooden stage.

In that moment, with my square diploma turned to face the camera, my equally square mortarboard sitting stupidly atop my
~~~

head, I'm sure I felt triumphant. Happy. I'm sure I believed my accolades, my academic successes, had granted me some kind of agency, just as I believed I had gained power by divorcing sex from want, physical intimacy from emotional trust. I'm sure I felt, in that moment, that the ground was firm beneath me. My standing secure. My gaping want concealed.

Fifteen years later, I am reconsidering this image of myself with closer attention. I am looking at the figure in question: my body, how she moves and waves and thinks within the confines of that stage, that space. How she was raised, and how her efforts at rebellion all remained within the borders, against the floorboards, that contextualized her existence. I look, and I see the cost—of my assumptions, my miscalculations, my state of high, my state of repression. I see a woman who is at once exposed and trying to hide. Who is only semiconscious.

DOUBLE EXPOSURE

Her face shines out from piles of records stacked in plastic crates, one arm wedged against pillared vinyl and dust. The photograph is black and white. You can't discern the reddish tinge of her hair, just the heavy bangs across her brow. She is smiling. It is hard to see, without the variance of color and light, what kind of smile.

It is one of the only photographs he takes of her during their short relationship, an image snapped on a day spent wandering the streets of San Francisco, a day after a party.

The party is in January. She has just turned twenty-three. The bangs are new. The man who takes her picture will soon tell her, "I don't want anything serious," and she will say, "Then neither do I." For the first and only time in her romantic life, she will mean those words down to her bones.

~~~

I have a sense that it began with the bangs. I don't mean the fact of them, that they changed me somehow. Rather, the decision to cut
~~~

them in—heavy and blunt, like Grace Slick's, after having always had long, face-framing layers, soft around my cheeks—was an external commitment to the internal self I intended to cultivate.

In this way, the version of myself first captured in that photograph and several others like it from that San Francisco winter, January 2008, is the fledgling version of a self that would persist throughout my early twenties: from Berkeley and San Francisco to Baja, back to the city and then up and down, up and down the California coast.

This self was a different self from the woman I'd been, all cooped up and turtlenecked and lovelorn, in my last collegiate Vermont winter. That woman sparked and rumbled. She was angry, sharp, ambitious. Eager for affection but cynical, even as she harbored ideals about transcendence from the everyday of gendered squabbling to something mythic, or even better.

She—that is, I (for the twenty-two-year-old was, I think, much closer in many ways to the elemental self I am or carry with me, that I identify with now, though of course I carry all of these selves in some form or another)—had spent that final year immersed in the lives and letters and poems and Zen pursuits of the Beat and San Francisco Renaissance poets. Of these, she made a close study of one poet in particular: Joanne Kyger, a precocious child author turned aspiring writer from her own hometown (or nearly—the town just next to hers), who moved to San Francisco in 1957 and became central to the North Beach scene. Vesuvio's. City Lights. Gallery Six.

Years later, I would marvel at the mimicked cadence of my written journals from this time: the linguistic scrapbooking, à la Kyger, of domestic and critical, poetic and philosophical and sexual ephemeral peppered across page after page of lined Moleskine notebook paper. I would observe my uncharacteristic decision to take a Buddhism course (the only one in which I earned, I think, a *B* instead of an *A* throughout my college career—telling, perhaps, in retrospect), my more logical choice of yoga and meditation PE classes (easy credit, good for stress). I would notice habits that began in those Kyger-steeped months—lining my lower eyelids with black kohl pencil, my ubiquitous black turtlenecks, a propensity to drink wine from coffee mugs or jelly jars—as direct imitations of images and descriptions of Joanne and her cohort in late 1950s North Beach poetry salons.

Kyger's early poems, her journals from the early 1960s, and her personal letters and postcards detailing the five years she spent married to the Beat icon Gary Snyder and living in Japan lay at the core of my senior thesis project. They also reached into the core of me—my language, habits, yearnings—and I welcomed them, wove them into my sense of self.

~~~

By March, the San Francisco man will have changed his mind. About seriousness. About the girl with the bangs. He will realize, after she has been gone for a month, that he misses her. Even go so far as to leave a handwritten, hand-illustrated letter and a small bundle of wildflowers at her doorstep, to be found upon her arrival home from Mexico.

But it will be too late. And in fact, it was already too late, that moment—in his Airstream in Santa Cruz, beneath the redwoods, their bodies sprawled on a pile of fuzzy woolen blankets, the warm low-lit glow of the trailer perfectly romantic—when he balked at commitment.

Besides, by March, she'll have met A.

Like the man from San Francisco, A will take her picture. This time, there will be many photographs: her pale limbs gone sun-gold, her bare toes, her blunt bangs growing out, clustering within and against her lashes. Skin ruddied with sun, skin unaccustomed to so much heat in February. She will feel tan and pretty opposite his lens; but in the photos, when I look back at them years later, her face will be red, red, her eyes tiny and blue, her cheeks shining.
~~~

They will meet at a yoga teacher training in Baja, a twenty-three-day residential immersion at the beach. She'd requested airfare and tuition for the trip as a graduation present. The yoga retreat had seemed like an ideal reset after all of the heady, boozy, anxious celebrations she'd just left behind at college. In Mexico, she imagined, she would eat vegetarian food and give up coffee and alcohol (except on Sundays, when everyone would travel to the nearby town and gorge on fresh flour tortillas and margaritas and buckets of hot coffee with cream). She would sleep in a tent with a mattress but no mirrors. She would have room to pack only a few books and no makeup. And while she couldn't know for certain, she'd suspect there wouldn't be any—or many—men at this retreat.

She'll be right. There will be about twenty women, and only two men. One of them will be A.

Telling the story in the years that followed, she and A would laugh: about how wholly different they were when they first met, about how unlikely such a pairing seemed—to them, to everyone at the yoga camp. That's what they called it afterward, with endearment: "yoga camp." A, with his high and tight haircut only just beginning to grow out after a recent separation from the armed forces, his tidy beard, his body always dressed in branded athletic shorts and zip-up track jacket. Her, my self-in-transition, slow to relinquish her hard-won academic accolades and arch manners but trying earnestly with slower speech and American Apparel green yoga pants that flared and a beaded string bracelet on her wrist and those thick bangs.

But within a few days, she'd felt it: an electric current of pleasure at his incidental touch, immediately followed by the heat of despair when that touch, those hands, met the hands of other young women—Emily, Rachel, Angela, Sienna—instead of hers. The horror, when she recognized this feeling: jealousy, desire. That such an attraction should mar the peace of this, her intended experiment with celibacy and spiritual growth. That such jealousy should invade even the simple innocence of a mindfulness exercise in which everyone held hands with everyone else.

In her limited experience, it didn't seem tenable to have both. To entertain a crush while likewise focusing on something as nebulous and tender as her ego, her nascent selfhood.

~~~

The Tapestry and the Web was Kyger's first published collection of poems, a series blending epic surreality, domestic sketches, and revisionist takes on *The Odyssey*'s Penelope as a more powerful, possibly devious agent against patriarchy. As Kyger writes in "Pan as the son of Penelope":

> Some thing keeps escaping me. Something
> About the landing of the husband's boat upon the shore.
>
> She did not run up and embrace him as I recall.
> He came upon her at the house & killed the suitors.
> *I* choose to think of her waiting for him
> Concocting his adventures bringing
> The misfortunes to him
> —she must have had her hands full.

At twenty-two, I adored this poem, this postulation: of the ever-patient wife reclaiming power as an agent of chaos, of the poet wielding her imagination on the page with such assurance. I was also romantically and sexually frustrated, desirous of a partner despite myself, and hungry for any art, music, or literature geared toward the more vengeful modes of feminism. I listened to a lot of Tori Amos and Fiona Apple and wrote blatantly imitative Edna St. Vincent Millay–inspired poetry (the snarky kind). Situated within this milieu, and being as they were (at that time, anyway) only
~~~

superficially explored by literary scholars, Kyger's Penelope poems seemed the perfect fit for a thesis topic.

As much as I admired Kyger's power and subversive approach to myth, I could also see past the more immediate pleasures of her poetry to something larger that, I felt certain, she was trying to achieve—out of poetry, out of life. Something that I was striving for, too. My working thesis, developed during the same semester as the Buddhism class, challenged established scholarly readings of *Tapestry* as a primarily gendered, proto-feminist project. Instead, I argued, Kyger wanted to "transcend" the identifying limitations of gender—an idea I might now describe as "queering the Penelope myth"—and seek a "universalized" poetic ideal, one in which "control" and victory elude both male and female entities and humility wins the day.

This "universal" postulation haunts me now, at least in terms of word choice, as it is the exact language that has since come to frustrate so many female and nonbinary academics and authors—myself included—writing from the heart of lived and embodied experience, only to be urged away from personal particularity toward "the universal" (that is, patriarchal, objective, sanctioned by structures and systems of power). Then, as now, I couldn't unsee the importance of the individual, the domestic, and the particular in Kyger's poetic. I didn't attempt to. But I wanted to reach beyond what I still considered, at that time, to be "the feminine sphere," to suggest the universalist import of these details. And in 2007, I was reaching half-blind. I had only taken one catch-all introduction to literary theory, the kind taught by an old-guard white dude who rendered feminist thought a micro-blip on the syllabus, and I had been intrigued but overwhelmed by the supplemental readings, featuring the likes of Butler and Kristeva, that had popped up in my "Irish Women Writers" course at Trinity. How differently I might have approached Kyger's writing had I regarded those readings with closer attention, or had I known to bring Audre Lorde or Adrienne Rich or Alicia Ostriker into the mix.

Looking back, I believe I wanted to see Kyger as succeeding in her no-self errand, her poetic Buddhist ideal, on the first attempt. I may also have misread—or read to the advantage of my specific angle (as most of us do, at one time or another)—the relevant *Tapestry* poems and personal fragments I included in my paper. But most importantly, I wanted to see some hope for a less embattled relationship between men and women, and my youthful romanticism, no matter how deeply and heavily I mired it in multivalent sentence structures and original research and persnickety syntactical parsings, was determined, in the end, to have its way.

~~~

In Mexico, she and A kept finding themselves thrown together. Sometimes she instigated these encounters; at other times, she began to suspect, they were his doing. Then the two of them were named *satya* partners—everyone at camp was paired off for this assignment, committed to telling the truth to one another, to creating a space for judgment-free intimacy throughout the training—and it became clear that their attraction, connection, was apparent to (and seemingly sanctioned by) their instructors and peers.

After the first *satya* session, it was only a matter of time before he asked her to take a walk on the beach. When they kissed beneath the moonlit palms, she laughed with incredulity, with joy.

The next day, she tried to meditate on her ego: that ambition, competitive desire, anger, fire in her mind she'd felt in the chill of Vermont, in the face of her thwarted desires. This might be the answer, she thought, lying prone on her yoga mat in the thatched open-air studio during instruction. To let it all go. To be a body, first; mind, second. To stop fighting so hard to be the smartest and the best. To seek balance through connection with another.

That night, she and A found one another in the tents. They talked and kissed for hours, but agreed not to have sex, at least not at
~~~

first, and this made her feel safe and open with him. The very next night, perhaps in part because of such a conversation—vulnerable, trusting—they couldn't keep their hands, tongues, skin off one another. They were in her tent. She felt him hard against her, her own desire so palpable it might have been an accident—the thrust that took him all the way inside. Except it wasn't an accident. He thrust again.

She could not, in those few quick seconds, reconcile desire, resistance, worry, pleasure, surprise. She could not, in the days and years that followed, remember if he'd said something afterward, or what exactly she had said or not said in response, before they carried on. All she knew was that it had happened unexpectedly. That the memory of that first time with A held within its beauty and eroticism a tiny, dark specter of unwanting; of choicelessness; of danger.

But that night, and every day and night and afternoon and morning after, she pushed that darkness from her mind. And with it buried, she seemed to find a second body hiding underneath her cold, black-clad, fearful, thinking body. A body in which every encounter could be unbridled, passionate. In truth, and with the passing of the days and weeks, her actual body peeled down: more muscle, more flex, more alive to pleasure. Her mind less anxious, busy. Some of this was the yoga. Some of this was the sunshine. Some of it was the limited intake of substances—alcohol, caffeine. But most of it was a first love combined with intense intimacy, an intimacy that seemed equal in its physical and emotional depth. In sum, a state she had never felt before. A state she imagined at once impossible to maintain and worth all imaginable sacrifice, compromise, to keep.

~~~

". . . and so help me this is the truth [I] got TRICKED into getting married."

So wrote Kyger in her journals as soon as she arrived in Kyoto, Japan, to live with Snyder in 1960—the marriage, a necessary
~~~

formality for cohabitation in Kyoto, but one that Kyger hadn't necessarily agreed to prior to making the trip. Her journals and letters dating from the Kyoto years provide a very personal perspective on her difficulty with juggling affection, partnership, Zen, poetry, and patriarchy.

"What do I think I will lose.—afraid of being over powered," she wrote in the next day's journal entry. Several years later, in a letter to her friend Philip Whalen: "I have an ego . . . problem: an awful superiority complex and an awful inferiority complex and no balance." That she was seeking balance despite these problems, I'd argued back in college, set her apart. Her self-awareness. Her desire to find her place within the tricky, overlapping both-and of femininity and masculinity, of ego and renunciation, of poetic power and enlightenment.

But the search was fraught. Snyder had distinct ideas—"Gary Snyder's Plan"—about a wife and home and gender roles and behavior. What's more, Joanne had just been coming into her own as a poetry hotshot in the San Francisco scene when she left, whereas in Kyoto she was reduced to being a wife. Snyder, meanwhile, was already world-renowned. Her choice to live with him, then, was a sacrifice of her own rising star—not to mention her autonomy. The tone of her letters and journals alternated (oftentimes rapidly) between incredulousness, anger, acid sarcasm, tenderness, petulance, and contrition. And regardless of how it was expressed, her preoccupation throughout was fueled by indignant and frustrated rebellion against the subservience that Snyder and society alike demanded of her: "a real *fear* of being submerged, not heard."

Kyger proceeded to move in and out of her own private life and her shared domestic life with Snyder: together and separate, they'd cook dinner or sit in meditation or host guests. Joanne would arrange flowers, go to the market, wash dishes, mix a drink—gin, jam, soda, lemon. She'd write in her journal, write to the cat, sketch out her poems. She'd try to be the wife Snyder had in mind for himself, for herself.

"It is conceivable," she noted, several months into the marriage, "that one could be in love with a person yet not able to live with them. About half the time my mind is concerned with getting away from him, he drains me. It seems to me half the time our relationship is involved in a battle to see who is going to get the upper hand. But when we balance, all is beautiful."

~~~

Things moved quickly after yoga camp. My new self, wholly besotted with A, immediately began planning a visit to see him in Hawaii. Once she arrived, they drank mai tais on the beach and fell asleep in the sun and smoked weed in a hammock for days in a row. Back in California, she kept a similar schedule: did yoga every day and smoked a little weed each afternoon before walking around Berkeley, often to the Whole Foods Market for free samples—grazing—then back again to stretch her body, feel it, revel in its flex and arch, her head a little light and loose. She was living off savings from the paralegal job she'd taken during that first summer after college. She was enjoying, for the first time she could remember, a life free from academic or professional commitments. It was an easy time to be in love, to let that love and resultant feelings of openness and somatic freedom envelope her days. To amplify said freedom with a perpetual mild high: marijuana in the afternoons, a beer or two each evening.

A came to visit her and stayed. The two of them moved in with a friend in San Francisco for the summer, a writer friend from college. She didn't write. Instead, she and A did yoga in the living room and wandered near the ocean or the Haight or went to Vesuvio's for wine. She lost interest in graduate school. Put it off indefinitely. A moved back home to his family's house in Texas and she pined. They wanted to be together but didn't know where or how, what to do for money. Then she found a conference center in South Lake Tahoe hiring seasonal workers for room, board, and minimum wage.
~~~

Both applied: her for a kitchen job, him for dining room service and security. August 2008. The last season, as it happens, that the conference center would hire inexperienced staff—stoners, nomads, over-educated twentysomethings—before the recession made it an essential source of employment. Only in hindsight would they realize their privilege, their luck.

They packed their bags into her Volvo station wagon and drove north. Lived together in a cabin on the lake, a tiny dank and dingy place that she adorned with thrift-store paintings, that they both stunk up with incense and marijuana on their nights off. If the work wasn't easy for her—she'd never had a service job like this before, only office assistantships, and had to learn so many things: how to slash apart an eight-piece chicken, stabilize a cutting board, deep-clean an industrial oven—she was also enamored with the physicality of it all. The mindfulness of moving, chopping, scrubbing, even plucking stems off baby spinach for a fancy wedding party. All of it, so new to this: her body, all of its openness. A served meals and watched for bears at night. Their lives felt elemental, of the moment.

Even as the autumn turned, the conference center maintained a summer camp energy. In the evenings, everyone took home the leftover open wine from dinner service and made a bonfire by the water or gathered in one of the larger cabins to play music. Everyone was young. Everyone had a guitar or weed or both. Everyone got high. Easy work, and pleasure.

She liked the parties and loved the toughened feeling that bristled her forearms and fingertips. She became enamored of the sweet ache: of cheap whiskey, pan burns, and knife scars. Of dildos, silk ropes, soft whips in black leather.

Tahoe is a strange paradise. It couples the natural beauty and ski culture of the Sierras with the libidinous opportunism of Las Vegas. The lake is like a diamond. The fanciest casino, at least back in 2008, was the MontBleu—a neon tower of icy silver and glass. Sex boutiques and wedding chapels appeared along Highway 50 intermixed with ski rental services, craft breweries, snowboard repair, vegan cafes. At the sex shop near their apartment, the apartment they rented together after the seasonal job ended and they both got winter gigs in town, A bought her a vibrator. Her first. He introduced her to so many things she'd never tried before, never thought to try or could imagine she might like. Soft leather and intricate bondage, mirrored hotel ceilings and the pleasure of being filmed—the two of them knowing they were watching in the future even as they tangled up with one another in the present, every now and then turning to the camera, to watch its blinking light.

As the self reflected in those mirrors, those photographs, the body enveloped in A's brown arms and silky white ropes, she desired what was happening because it was happening with A. She wanted to be open. She wanted to explore. Later, I would come to recognize this exploratory openness as, at least in part, what Maggie Nelson describes in *On Freedom* as "emergent desire" or "a certain fissured sovereignty, one that lessens the burden of always having to keep one's guard up . . . or even having to know if, not to mention what, one desires." I would realize this "fissured sovereignty" as something all my selves have sought, over and over and over again—via intimacy, or via alcohol, and all too often with an effort to achieve the former with help from the latter. But I would also have to contend with the fact that the self I was with A in those early years wanted, most of all, to want what *he* wanted. To be—not just sexually, but *actually*—what he wanted her to be. To make whatever compromise, sacrifice, if it might sustain that unprecedented intimacy she'd first felt with him back in Mexico.

Sometimes she didn't know what he wanted and tried to guess. Sometimes she felt a reflexive distaste for his requests. When this happened, she'd try to push the reflex from her mind.

She didn't always realize that, of course, he could tell when she recoiled. That he was right there, too, inside the mirror, image, film. That he had been there, noticed, that first night they'd slept together, likely regretted the failed communication as much as she had (and indeed, eventually, after their breakup, would say as much). That the depth of intimacy went both ways. That he wanted to maintain that intimacy, too, wanted her to want him back with all that passion she was feeling, and every time she flinched, she inflicted a new wound.

Only in hindsight would they realize their mutual capacity, in so much loving, to cause harm.

~~~

What to say about A. In so many ways—both the very best and the very worst—I soon realized he was a lot like my mother. Creative. Capable of great anger and great joy. Deeply desirous of intimacy. Deeply troubled, depressed, and suffering from the commingled effects of toxic masculinity and compounded trauma, a state that made alcohol and pot medicinal at best and requisite at worst. He was handsome and artistic. He rode a motorcycle with extreme care and made homemade sugar water for the hummingbirds. He wanted a new life after the military. What kind of life, he didn't know.

Different or not, we'd found a pool of conversant wants and needs and hopes between us in those *satya* conversations, in our love-starved bodies. After, in our companionable drinking and utopian, pseudo-hippy ideals. No one besides my mother had ever loved me as fiercely as A. Such a fearful magnitude of love. I didn't know how to repay it, other than to be and do everything I could to fill him up with sweetness in return.

But this is not an essay about A. Not really. And it is not, in the end, about how our lives progressed, or how our respective ambitions and realizations slowly pulled us apart. It is not an accusation or a confession of wrongdoing. And it is not an essay about Kyger, either—though I will admit to having missed her, to having enjoyed revisiting her words and character and voice.

What I am trying—needing—to do in writing these things down together, in putting all of these memories and images of "me" and
~~~

"her," of Kyger and A, of all our multiple selves side by side or over and under, layered together, is to see and understand, at once enliven and detach from, that version of myself that cut my bangs and didn't cling to the San Francisco man and instead met A and fell in love and let herself fall all the way into a depth of intimacy she'd never allowed herself before or permitted since. I am trying to recognize the things she compromised and sacrificed, believing that she needed to in order to achieve and keep that love. To look back upon those moments of emergent desire and realize how they became formative in her understanding—sometimes wrong, sometimes right—of her own, my own, innate desire. And to identify, if possible, those moments when the compromise and sacrifice began—and what it was, in yielding to that sacrificial impulse, she felt the need to give up.

There is one such moment I remember with a maddening blend of clarity and fog. It is a moment I buried many times over because I didn't want to either place or take responsibility for what happened afterward, a moment submerged beneath the memories of things that will always be beautiful, things for which I will always be grateful: like when A bandaged my hand after I cut myself with a bread knife at the Blue Angel Café in Tahoe and soothed me, wrapping my arm in a makeshift sling fashioned from my scarf; or when he would drive with me to visit my mother in Chino several years after my parents' separation and stay through even the most difficult times—when her extended hospitalization and hospice after precautionary chemotherapy and radiation for a tiny carcinoma utterly destroyed her already-damaged intestines and she needed two months to recover; or when a persistent cough the following year led doctors to believe that maybe that tiny cancer had metastasized to her lungs (it hadn't), and we hovered for a week waiting for the test results. All the times he'd held me close when I needed him or drove when I was too afraid to hold the wheel or wanted me when I felt unwantable.

And yet this moment remains. Asserts itself relentlessly when

I ask, of my memory, of my younger self and the magic she and A once shared: Where did she go? Where have they gone?

It must have been after Tahoe. Maybe 2009. She and A were back in San Francisco, at a party. A birthday party for her college friend, the Turkish writer who not long after would move to Paris and become a celebrated novelist. But before Paris, the Turkish writer and her partner lived in Palo Alto, where he was studying at Stanford. This couple had invited them, my other self and A, for dinner once. The four had talked all night, drinking wine, peeling oranges, falling asleep on the cushioned floor. In the morning, the writer made perfectly imperfect scones and coffee. Everything she touched felt like a fairytale.

So when this woman sent an invitation to her birthday dinner at an Italian restaurant in North Beach, my self with the reddish hair and bangs (growing out a little, parted down the middle) felt excited and alive. It was a charmed commingling of everything she loved all at once: a reunion with several other college classmates relocated to the Bay, with the Turkish writer and her partner (with whom A had struck up a strong camaraderie), and with the North Beach of her literary fantasies. She'd dressed for the party with care, perhaps consciously reviving a little of her former Kyger-infused aesthetic: short skirt, black netted tights, black flats, seventies sweater jacket. A took her picture as they wandered near the restaurant. In this picture, she is facing away from him, peering into a darkened shop window. Standing on her toes. The mess of her upswept hair glints in the light of a streetlamp. The sweater jacket covers most of the skirt, emphasizing the length of her thighs and calves. In the darkness of the window, her face—eyes—are just a blur of light.

The dinner itself was urbane and heady and uncomfortable. There were lots of people, most of whom she didn't know or at least did not know well. There was also lots of wine, house red in big carafes. She drank heavily and fast to ease her nervous energy, then searched for commonalities from college, from Vermont—shared professors, dorms—with the former classmates at the table. A had volunteered to drive, so he sipped his single beer quietly and slowly. She saw his unease, but as the night wore on, she had begun—with the help of wine and reminiscence—to enjoy herself. She carried on, getting louder, swapping stories of academic conquests and gossip about famed faculty and books assigned and loved and loathed and with all of it, more wine, but in a way that felt like a release of something taut inside—a pinched muscle, finally rubbed loose. She loved to talk like this with other readers, with people who loved the things she loved.

After, walking to the car, A was very quiet. She asked him what was on his mind.

"I didn't like you like that," he said.

A wave of shame washed over her. She felt, in his long silence leading up to these words and then the words themselves—short, terse—a heavy guilt. Confirmation, she supposed, that he was right. That she had let her ego crawl back up her throat—gossiping, vying—and looked ugly to him in the restaurant light. That her inside references and jokes must have seemed pretentious. Maybe even cruel.

In that instant, wine-buzzed and heartbroken and terrified that she might lose him, she promised not to be "like that" ever again. She didn't ask him to elaborate. Somewhere inside, her understanding of what he meant by "like that" merged a great many things—gossip, ego, privilege, yes, but also intellectualism, ambition, politics, criticism, feminism even—into a single unwieldy ball. All of it, to eliminate; bury; sacrifice in pursuit of her better self, her sweetest self. The self, she thought, who could be loved.

~~~

"Do I feel subdued and purged. Or is it only hair pushed back from my forehead in a new style."

So wrote Joanne—in a statement, not a question, perhaps the truest way of describing this, the peculiar effect a change in life
~~~

and a change in hair can have on one's sense of newness. I could call this a piece of gendered minutiae, a "feminine" observation . . . but that would be a lie.

The entry is dated January 3, 1964. Her resolutions for the new year were all about poetry: "The craft should fit like a glove. Exactly: from my *own* life, not sources from myth." Within two weeks, she would board a ship back to San Francisco, taking her typewriter and her new hair. Writing a last letter to Gary. Writing down her dreams:

> Gary merging into my mother. Then detaching and remaining separate in the background. While I have a dream in which Mother is running a boarding house. I demand a separate room from the house. Which I get and fix up.
>
> He wouldn't let me keep a wooden spoon.

Her final *Tapestry* poem, "From our soundest sleep, it ends," dates almost a year exactly from the writing of this dream sketch, the last in a series presaging the divorce from Snyder. In this poem, "She"—Kyger, Penelope—"finished up the web."

"It has been difficult to write this," she said. "Why they must go to war I can't decide." In my undergraduate thesis, I suggested that the final battle scene in which Persephone yields control to "man" and "control takes peace / over an ordered landscape" represents humility on the part of the goddess and a renunciation of gendered dualities. The evidence is there throughout the book, but so, too, is that of a disappointment, a reckoning with loss and regret. I don't talk about this loss, this failure, in my essay. I do not address the last two lines of the poem.

In these lines, Kyger wrote, "It is clear / all confusion gone, and nodding their heads wondered where they had gone." Rereading the poems and my critical response, I'm a little surprised my advisor let me get away with this oversight. Sure, it's handy to end on "peace / over an ordered landscape," but who the hell is this conclusive "they"? What, in fact, is now "clear"? Are the nodding heads moving in assent, or in nods of bewilderment? So much, it seems, is now "gone" (twice!).

Where had they gone? Where had they gone?

I imagine Kyger shaking her own head, putting a coda on this—her life with Snyder, her poetic experiment with myth, her attempt to "have it all" before Western society caught up with her ambition and began telling women everywhere that they not only *could* but *should*. Her reaching: for domestic bliss and dharma, a poetic voice and egolessness. Her love for Snyder and that "balance" they would strike, every now and then, that was so "beautiful" amid the rollicking fights and snarky letters back and forth to one another.

Most of the photographs in *Strange Big Moon: The Japan and India Journals* are taken from a distance. They show Joanne and Gary together on a Honda bike, at parties, exploring India with Allen Ginsberg. But there's one close-up portrait from that India trip: of Kyger in a squat, wearing threadbare flip-flops, pale leggings, and a black tunic dress. A scarf around her neck. Her bangs are heavy and flat above her eyes. She is cooking something over a tiny fire. The photo is in black and white. She is looking up at the camera—at Gary. Mouth half open. It is hard to see, without the variance of color and light, whether she is smiling or trying to speak.

Without wholly realizing it, I mimicked this outfit in Mexico. Our last night at yoga camp, I wore a black scoop-neck tunic and my green leggings. A copper scarf around my neck. Over and over, A took my picture.

I believe my self from that night, that time, thought ease and openness were things that, once found, she could capture and hold if she gave something up in exchange. It is troubling: how utterly divided I still feel, in many ways. How fully I believed, back then, I had to choose. How much I still struggle to believe the opposite.

After that night at the party in San Francisco, my selves slowly began to merge and jumble. A and I moved to San Diego, where I got a job writing sponsored content for a social media marketing firm. At night, I took creative writing classes. My bangs grew out, long and soft around my face again. The red dye faded completely.

These days, I often joke to my students—when telling stories about my old marketing career or breaking the ice in an introductory creative writing class with "two truths and a lie"—that I have had "a whole other life" before academia. When I think about it, I realize this is not a joke. Nor is it a "different" or a "former" life. Just a first one. An exposure at once past and parallel, the same strip of film run twice through the camera.

It is easy to forget—then, now—when looking at the photographs of Kyger from *Strange Big Moon*, how soon thereafter she sailed back home again, alone.

INTERLUDE: MILK CLOCK

2010

There are animals who eat their young. Hamster mothers do, apparently. And sometimes hens. Something to do with nutrients, a lack of calcium.

I do not often feel like I'm an animal. By that I mean I do not often feel like I am built, against some crisis, to survive.

When I wait too long to eat, my head feels loose: a baby tooth. Unseen hands, slackening the root. Slip a shiver more, and I might fall away. I'm accustomed to this hunger. Maybe it should scare me, but it's in my bones. What frightens me is others' hunger—that which I am bound to feed. Or possibly the hunger of a tiny someone, so brand new she doesn't know it yet—the scale. Her place, or where she'll fall among the animals.

It's springtime. Yosemite. Fields of almond, corn, and fig. A's cousin's wife, Maria, holding court—under backyard tents, under the waxing heat. She talks of nearly bleeding out after her second son was born. I stand a little distance off—chilled bottle of Corona to my wrist, hot stars behind my eyes. Maria laughs, resplendent in a fuchsia dress. I watch her lips, purple like the plump black-purple figs gone sun-ripe in the orchard. Watch her as she speaks: about the blood that soaked the sheets, blood and water in the shower, blood that dripped and pooled against the cracked linoleum. I watch the curve of her black hair, her brimming hips.

"Of course," she says, "when I got pregnant for a third time, I was nervous."

That's when I stand up—"Excuse me"—and move east. Past the cousins as they listen. Past their waiting eyes and paper plates weighed down with chili-reddened meat and macaroni salad. Past Maria's children as they eat carnitas, as they shove each other in the rented bounce house. Past her smile as she watches them, Corona bottle slick with sweat against her nails. Vermillion, shellac.

I make it to the east side of the house, then turn the corner. Suck the sweet of shade-chilled air, then hold it. Bend.

After, I go looking for the kittens: five strays that hide and scratch and scamper in the eaves of this old house. Night after night, we hear them: A and I, asleep beneath the oak and metal-mounted buck's head, gutted eyes gone black as hills.

I find them mewing in the moonlight, their heads poked out above the once-white, rust-red screen. Earlier this year, their mother disappeared. Vanished, and the aunties whispered—over Touched by an Angel, *over* Jerry Springer, *over coffee and pan dulce on the sofa—that she must have died. Hit by a car or caught by a coyote.*

What other explanation? Why else would she leave?

Tonight, I see her. The mother: tail alive and down. Hunting in the orchard. I do not tell.

I watch her as the big sky darkens. I duck in through the front door, pour two fingers of tequila into a water glass with ice. Watch her from the kitchen window, cool and safe inside, sweat drying and invisible against the cotton pine-dark of my cheap green dress.

I watch the tall grass quicken in the sunset wind. I watch the children, hungry from their bouncing, reach and grab into the foil tins of meat and beans and macaroni salad.

I mirror them; I reach. I reach and bring the glass up to my lips.

The heat and beer have loosened up my neck. I watch the cat move silent and away. I feel my ankle bones, cold and solid underneath my skin. Until she disappears. And then I drink.

STILL LIFE

Sometimes, out of nowhere, I see myself small—three years old, maybe four. The same image arises repeatedly. It is an old image, taken from my parents' first house, the brown stucco duplex in the small suburban town northeast of San Francisco. I see myself lying on the well-worn Persian rug in our living room, a rug that always seemed to me like an ocean. It was an inverse island, all my own and yet mere steps away from the kitchen, my favorite room in the house. A white Polaroid frame holds the image still in my imagination, gives my memory a border, a shape. It bathes recollection in sepia, turning my pale skin rosy, my brown hair golden. When I see this image, I return to the living room, to the rug. I remember how it felt to roll my body across the soft fibers, to lie in a pool of afternoon light.

I was strangely shaped as a child, sporting a bulging belly and scant hair well past toddlerhood. Later, we'd realize I was probably sensitive to many foods: milk, corn, soy. All the "healthy" foods my mother had fed me, foods I'd eaten with gusto. By the age of two,

I had what looked like a beer gut (not from beer; probably from dairy). By the age of ten, semipermanent dark circles under my eyes.

I used to swim this ungainly body around on the paisley expanse of the rug, imagining myself into seafaring adventures. My mother loved classical composers, especially Satie and Stravinsky. She would put a record on and pour herself a glass of wine in the late afternoons and I would writhe and flop and wiggle around in time to the music. Coming out of the kitchen to join me, she would sit on the couch and listen as I recounted the day's exploits among pirates or mermaids. Some days, she'd even get down onto the rug with me and play along.

"Where are the pirates, captain?" she might say, in all seriousness. "What is your plan of escape?"

"Not pirates," I'd gasp as I floundered, fighting amongst the crashing waves. "Not pirates but fish men, they are coming for the princess, and I must protect her."

"Would the captain like some juice before setting sail again?" my mother might ask, after a while.

Mom had studied fine art in undergrad and started a master's at Otis College back when she lived in Los Angeles, back when she made money waiting tables at Bruno's Italian restaurant and temping at the Solid Gold production studio in its early heyday. These may have been concurrent jobs, or successive jobs. She tells the stories in a web of spirals, each spinning out and back to the nexus of her youth, the youth before I lived, but the loops never quite line up. The story changed. The story changes. All I know for certain is what she wore and looked like, from the photographs. What she made and sketched and painted—just a fraction of her art, from the work she saved.

Back then, my mother wore her wavy dark-brown hair down past her shoulders. Her jeans were flared and high at the waist, her skin a light olive, her blouses invariably sexy no matter how oversized or masculine in cut. Her college boyfriend, Steve—the only one, to my knowledge, without a nickname, the only one she still considers a friend—had red hair in a braid and a bushy mustache, green-and-white-checked polyester pants and an arm around my mother in every photograph. Much later, she would tell me how they had lived together in a tiny apartment in Echo Park; how he would drive her broken-down Volkswagen with wooden bumpers to a coffeehouse near MacArthur Park for coffee and cheese danish, then drop her off at Otis while he installed fire doors in an old brick flophouse; how they'd make short films for class and go watch Charlie Chaplin retrospectives at the Los Feliz Theater; how they named their cat Ubu after the Dadaist masterpiece they both worshiped in the early 1970s.

She would tell me about her sculpture teacher, Renzo Fenci, an Italian ex-pat who would make a name for himself with a series of Brutalist figure sculptures dotted across the greater Los Angeles area as curb appeal for the now defunct Homes Savings and Loan chain of banks. She would tell me how Renzo doted on a very young, very pretty girl in their class at Otis, a girl whom my mother saw as lacking in real talent. She would tell me how her experience in Renzo's class and in art crit with this particular young woman would come to limit her sense of female artistic friendship during college; how her only real art friend, in fact, was Steve.

My mother used trash and oil cans to inspire abstract canvas paintings for her classes. She didn't call herself a feminist. She and Steve created short films in which my mother—in full makeup and kimono, holding a pair of Japanese wooden figure dolls together in the palm of one hand—would emerge from a closet, gesture suggestively, and then retreat. No sound. Just her eyes, her hair, her hands. Steve winking behind the camera.

While I was growing up, my mother's artwork took up two of the four walls in our small living room. There was a sweeping, nameless, blue-green spacescape of a painting—one of the two "trash can paintings," as she would later call them—and a still life in charcoal, all starkness and shading, graphite and gray. From my vantage point on the rug, the painting was like a canopy, opening into a world of unknowns. Strips of steely silver slit the waves of sea-foam green, with swaths of ethereal blues like windows. I didn't know about the trash cans or the art crits or the boyfriends then. Sprawled at my mother's feet, all I could see was that blue-green abandon. Meanwhile, the still life would stare down at us from above the piano, its precise lines and cavernous shadows hidden in the waning yellow light of coming dusk.

~~~

I'm twenty-five and getting ready, yet again, to move out of my parents' second house. The first move was for college; the second, after graduation, into a rented room in a converted purple Victorian on College Avenue in Berkeley, only about twenty minutes' drive west or a handful of stops on the BART train away. The third move—out to Tahoe with A—had been further but lower stakes, intentionally temporary, an exodus in search of seasonal employment in exchange for lakeside living free of rent. But this fourth move is for real. A and I had been living with my parents while looking for a place to settle more permanently and at last had found our perfect solution in the low rents and hippy vibes of Ocean Beach in San Diego, a kind of surfer's Haight-Ashbury equivalent known as "OB" by the locals, a place that embraced itinerant living and offered easy access to sand, saltwater, sunshine, and weed.

This move, in other words, feels adult. It warrants a U-Haul rental. We are taking furniture and dishes. It is the biggest move I've made yet, the most serious in terms of literal and figurative weight.

As I'm packing, I'm also taking stock of this house—not the house of the Persian rug and the Polaroid memories but a bigger, newer house that my parents bought when I was nine and furnished with plush pastel furniture, earmarks of mid-1990s middle-class aspiration. Downstairs, in the living room, the walls are decorated with purchased art prints—baroque flower arrangements and Renaissance angels—encased in filigreed faux-gold frames. Most
~~~

of the art I remember with that sepia-tinted nostalgia has been stuffed into hiding places: upstairs closets, under-bed drawers.

The painting is an exception. As I pack, I take the painting down, rolling it up, and the canvas coughs up dust, spewing it around the room. I've had it hanging over my bed ever since coming back the previous autumn. The deep blues are soothing, the gray slashes energetic, like slaps of cold seawater. In the new house, in the years prior to my return, Mom had kept the painting rolled up and tucked away in the garage. Only the still life had stayed in its frame, and even that had been relegated to the downstairs bathroom, the one we tended to neglect unless company was coming over. I remember that bathroom as a catch-all receptacle for oddities: spare hangers, unloved dog toys, backup plungers. We put everything into the unused tub, then pulled the shower curtain closed.

Mom is helping me pack. She isn't happy about the move.

"Would you be willing to let me take this painting with me?" I ask. "I'd like to have something of yours to hang up in the new place."

Mom looks at the canvas, inexpertly rolled and sitting limp on the carpet, blank side out, with only the slightest hint of blue peeping from behind the unfinished edges.

"You want that one?" she says. "I mean—sure, you can take it if you want. But it isn't any good."

I catch a sharpness in her voice but try, as I so often have, to smooth its edges with a positive tone and forced enthusiasm. "What? No way. I love it! It's amazing!"

Mom wrinkles her lips. "That painting is just artsy crap," she says. "It's based on a garbage can. Anyway, I was never good with abstract subjects."

This surprises me, and I lose some ground, realize I can't just compliment my way through the tension. I want to tell her that I like the painting, that I don't think it's crap. After all, I *do* like the painting, have always liked it. More than that, though, I want her to care what I think, even if my understanding of fine art is limited at best. But the prevailing elephant in the room is that I'm leaving her, and soon—known to me, unbeknownst to her—so will my father.

"You know the still life? The one in charcoal?" she says. "*That* one is good." She looks back at me now, gauging my response. I recall the mass of dark shapes crowding against one another. A city skyline in the fog with just a single peak here or cornice there still sharp enough to recognize.

"Yeah," I say, dumb and uncertain.

"You can't have it." This, she snaps at me. Automatically, I flinch.

"Your father doesn't give a shit about any of this, you know," she adds. "He never has."

~~~

It's winter in San Diego, and the sky is alternately slate gray or obscenely bright, mocking the instincts of the season, belying the chill in the wind. The days scoot forward slowly, and the waves are dull and flat, relentless in their failure to pound and roil in tempo with my moods. Mom calls daily. Dad moved out two weeks after A and I left. Now, after two months of my own feigned optimism and her indignant disbelief, it is clear to us both that he isn't coming back. Her voice is in my head every day, every night. I lie awake beside A under shafts of moonlight sliced through palm shadows. I listen to the airplanes take off and land, take off and land.

We have a dining nook in our apartment but no dining table. Instead, we put a thrifted coffee table painted green and blue and silver in the center of the space and make it a kind of altar: incense, crystals, a Ganesha figurine from World Market—all of this an aesthetic holdover from yoga camp as opposed to a genuine symbol of spiritual practice. But it is an altar to something. Maybe to love.

I hang the painting above the coffee table, hoping the piece of myself that I found in its depths will grace our new start. But when I get it up onto the wall, I realize that the colors have begun to fade.
~~~

Once, on a wet December night when A is out and I'm home alone, I sit on the living room floor and listen to Satie and Stravinsky on iTunes. The sound is tinny and flat piped through a laptop speaker. The apartment feels hollow.

Months stretch on. Mom keeps calling.

~~~

When I was about four years old, I drew a blue line in crayon on the white stucco wall of the downstairs hallway. The image is crisp inside me. I can, I am certain, still feel the sensation of the slim Crayola in my hand, the moment of impact; still see the lettering on the crayon denoting its color, "Cornflower Blue."

In my recollection of this moment, it was afternoon and sunny. The bright wall between the living room and the kitchen was totally blank, almost plaintive in its emptiness. I stood alone for a while, chubby-kneed and bare-legged, my droopy shorts hanging low beneath my rounded belly. I wrapped my fingers around the stem of the crayon in my hand. Slowly, with fear-tempered glee, I touched the crayon to the paint. I drew a dusky blue squiggle, a timid wave on a sea of white. The marking made it mine.

This, at least, is how I remember it. Years later, I asked my mom if she remembers, too. We were driving home from school, my mom behind the wheel of our faded yellow 1984 Volvo, me in the passenger seat. It was late afternoon in early fall, and the light was soaking in through the driver's side window, bathing Mom's hair, turning it auburn. I was probably about fourteen.

"Remember that time when I was a kid, when I drew on the wall?" I began, turning to face her as we made our way up a gentle hill. "I was, like, four, and I scribbled on the stucco with crayon?"

Mom yanked the gear shift and crinkled her brows. "You never drew on the wall, honey," she said. Her tone was calm, and a little confused.
~~~

"Like, you don't remember that I did? Because I'm pretty sure that I did," I pressed on, still looking at her face in the teething yellow light.

Mom turned the corner and the car passed beneath a tree. For a moment, we were covered in shade. Without looking at me, my mom shook her head. The shadows flickered through her hair.

"No. I just know it didn't happen." This time her voice was firm. "You never would have done something like that."

I blinked. Swallowed a stone. We turned again. This time, my face fell into the dark.

SEQUENCE OF EVENTS

This story is the hardest story to tell. It is hard because it happened long ago, in 2010, and even though I wrote in my journals at the time, wrote things down with more immediacy and clearer memory, it is impossible to fact-check my emotions. It is hard because my mother was so terribly angry and resentful then. She was angry at my father, angry at me, angry, I think, at her own parents and past lovers and absent friends, and her anger, as I see it now, seems to me so justified and yet so raw, so unbridled, so starved for validation. Her anger enveloped entire rooms; it haunted the dishwasher.

But this afternoon—this being 2021, eleven years after the events I will recount here—I am trying to decide how to tell it; seeking a way in. I walk downtown in the August heat, buy a string cheese and a bottle of water at the co-op market, then go to a tattoo appointment that lasts for nearly four hours. Lying on the table, I play this narrative, a narrative of illness and near-death, anger and abandonment, its iterations, over in my head. I talk to my tattoo artist, Karla: about Louise Bourgeois and John James Audubon, about museums and where to buy houseplants and the bleakness (her words, fully accurate) of online dating in this corner of the country. Of the bind within which we alike find ourselves: professionally successful artists, single women surrounded by perpetual man-boys and married couples, marooned in a charming, superficially progressive college town with a racist-sexist underbelly and a single male population obsessed with fishing, guns, and Seahawks football.

Then the conversation tapers, and Karla bends close against my skin to render shading, depth of weight to the reaching sagebrush trident stems and canopies of yarrow now strewn along my forearm. I close my eyes, ignore the hungry rumble in my stomach and the steel-wool rub of ink applied to skin.

The needle whirrs and my skin weeps. A loosening.

In 2010, I was as angry at my mother as she was with me. I often work now, as I did then, to hide my anger—from her, from everyone—because I find my mother's anger ugly and frightening, because I was taught by my father and the professional world that anger is unruly and bad. But my anger, and plenty of it, is still here. Buried, it spurts and spirals out in cruel and funny ways. Disallowed, it becomes a shapeshifter.

The truth is, my mother and I were not on good terms in 2010. I cannot write the story of her almost-death without reopening memories I have worked, via neglect, to render less potent. To get them back, I must confront the complicated feelings. Let them itch.

~~~

Mom bought the bell at an antique store on First Street, several weeks before she was scheduled to go in for surgery to correct a rectal prolapse. The appointment was to coincide with her fifty-ninth birthday. The bell was delicate: ceramic lace, painted a frosty pale green that reminded me of pistachio ice cream.

"If I'm going to be laid up on the couch after this operation, then I want to be treated like a queen." She started saying things like this to my father and me. "You two will be my servants and
~~~

you will do as I say." Then she'd ring the bell with a flick of her wrist, and it would tinkle obediently. "It's about time I got waited on, after all these years."

Dad would sigh. "I hardly think that will be necessary." In those days leading up to the surgery, his voice was dry and stern. He frequently retreated to the garage to watch football and ride the recumbent bike.

"I don't think either of you understands what this is going to be like, taking care of me, taking care of the house." Mom repeated variations on this theme over and over. "After the surgery, I won't be able to do anything. No lifting, no driving, no strain."

"I know, I know," I'd say, nodding. Mom hates it when I say *I know* in response to her suggestions, reminders, advice.

Throughout the day, Mom would reach to the low cabinet under the sink, the one where she stashed economy-sized bottles of Inglenook and Sutter Home white zinfandel, mini four-packs of Cook's champagne, the occasional fifth of vodka or Baileys. This habit, the stashing away of alcohol, wasn't new. But the volume seemed to have increased in recent months, the reaching more frequent.

Once, in the days leading up to the surgery, I'd asked her not to drink so much. Tried to tell her how it made me feel to watch. Her response, as I remember it, landed with near physical force against me:

"Shut the fuck up about how *you* feel," she'd said. "This is happening to me, do you understand? Me. Not to you, not to your father."

I opened my mouth to protest, but she cut me off.

"Just stop talking. You have to understand. Right now, I can't care about how you feel."

Looking back, I can only imagine. Her fear. My fear. The infinity loop of worry. Her need to not be a mother for once, to protect her own sanity and self. I can only imagine the urgency, the contradiction she must have felt in that moment: to be alone and yet cared for, permitted primacy in her need to survive. It is a need, in choosing not to have my own children, that I can now relate to in many ways. A compensatory shield.

But on that October morning, standing with my mother in the kitchen, I couldn't fathom anything beyond the hurt. The hurt and the guilt.

The initial laparoscopic surgery went as planned. Mom stayed in the hospital for three days. Dad and I took turns visiting. On the fourth day, Dad brought her home and we set her up on the couch with a sea of blankets, countless magazines, ready popsicles, the little bell. Within two days, she began experiencing sharp cramping in her abdomen. I remember being in the kitchen, scooping rainbow sherbet (a bizarre favorite of my mother's, then and now), when she called out.

Mom's face was pale, drawn with pain. Dad was at work. I suggested calling the doctor for advice. Mom said no. Instead, she asked for Vicodin. She could not, according to the prescription, have more for several hours.

"Please," she said. "It hurts."

I recited the doctor's strict warnings about dosage, specific to this type of surgery. The risk of slowing down the bowel with narcotics as it tried to heal.

"Listen," she interrupted. "Just bring me the goddamn pills. I'm lying here in pain, and you want to follow the rules? You want to be Little Miss Perfect?"

I had anticipated something like this, had even hidden the Vicodin in Dad's sock drawer and the Inglenook in my closet. But nothing could have prepared me for the gutted feeling her words hollowed out in me.

Eventually, I gave in.

By nightfall, we'd called 911. When the medics arrived, my mother was curled up on the floor by the front steps, my father and our dog Buster and I watching helplessly at her side. They took her away to the ER, where she was admitted and diagnosed with an obstruction, an intestinal blockage.

"This sort of thing is rare, but it can occur after abdominal procedures like hers," the doctor said. When we asked what might have caused it, he told us there were a variety of factors, ranging from simple scar tissue from the operation to improper eating habits during recovery. "And the Vicodin," he added, after a moment, looking thoughtfully at her chart. "That can certainly make things worse if taken to excess." He looked over his glasses at my mom, who nodded weakly. "We'll put you on something else while you're here, see if we can make things easier on your system."

I watched as he walked away, making little scribbles on his clipboard. I wanted to tell him what had happened, wanted—selfishly—for him to chasten her and exonerate me. To tell me that it wasn't my fault that Mom was back in the hospital. But instead I stayed quiet.

~~~

There is an Italian restaurant on the corner of Main and Sixth Streets here in downtown Moscow where my mother and I often meet to sit on the patio under the shade of orange umbrellas in the summer. It is her favorite, aside from the Mexican restaurant that is, as she puts it, "the only place in this town where they know how to make a *real* Long Island." After a week of heavy smoke and haze from the nearby wildfires and heat warnings across the Palouse, the weather breaks. There is a breeze, and clouds. Mom and I meet for an early supper of margherita pizza and salad. When I arrive, she is sipping a beer and flipping through "her Britain magazine," a large-format compilation of travel photos, museum stills, and ads for Viking cruises. I sit beside her in the shade, careful to keep my newly tattooed right arm out of the sun.

I've told my mom that I'm trying to remember things. The precise year it all happened, for example—I've managed to erase that part. Still holding the magazine in her lap, she recounts the timeline for me: surgery on October 30, 2010; at least three ER visits
~~~

thereafter, one of which I'd forgotten entirely; the Thanksgiving episode; my father's move-out date nearly one year later, on October 13, 2011.

"That's the date he put on all the divorce papers," she explains. "The date of 'the dissolution of our marriage.'"

We pretty much stop there, shift to discussing solutions for dry skin and summer razor burn. This recollecting is difficult: a little at a time is best. But on the following morning, Mom tells me she's been trying to get the timeline straight, writing things down.

"The psychotic episode makes a lot of the early stuff very disjointed," she writes in a text message. "Vivid memories, though. If you want to talk, I could come over in an hour."

When she arrives, we settle in my living room: her on the couch, me on the floor with my laptop on the coffee table. My cat Lou breathes softly, sleeping in a furry ball on the dark-blue, faux-midcentury-modern armchair in the corner. Every now and then we pause to watch her stretch, curl her sweet head upside down, reach her pink and black toes into the air. Otherwise, I let my mother speak. I listen and type. When she tells me she's struggling, asks me for a drink, I bring her a beer. It is 11 a.m., and I'm still in my pajamas (it's Saturday), but I understand.

What we cannot parse between the two of us is how it started: whether the epidural for her first surgery was the culprit, or if there was a second somewhere in that haze of ambulance trips and ER directives. My mother's guess is as good as mine: that in preparing for the initial surgery, the anesthesiologist (who later confessed to this) had struggled with the epidural, sending some of the drugs into my mother's spinal fluid and thereafter to her brain. Maybe it took a few days to land there because the first hospital stay was, according to all reports, as normal as can be. On this second stay, however, my mother started hearing things. First, it was a neighbor of ours, one who did, in fact, work at John Muir Hospital in Concord, where my mom had been admitted. Except she wasn't working at the time Mom heard her voice, heard her explaining that my dad wanted to bring Buster to the hospital to visit.

"I was in an old hospital bed with all those buttons and speakers, and none of them worked anymore," Mom says. "But I didn't realize and started screaming into the plastic at your father, 'Don't bring Buster, he will slip and fall on this slick floor! If you bring him here, I will divorce you!'"

After that, they moved Mom to a shared room. That is when the hallucinations began in earnest. My mother thought her roommate was having sex with strangers who came and went in the night, all to a radio soundtrack (there was no radio in the room), on repeat, of a jingle called "Happy Little Hobbit City." I wish I could render the tune, the tenor in which my mom re-creates the chords. It is at once mundane and horrifying, an earworm of the worst kind. With the hobbits in the background, my mother believed she was watching *David Letterman* on television—the opening credits, with exterior shots of the Ed Sullivan Theater—and that the building was covered in a sequin-studded net that had morphed through the TV screen, alternatively taking three-dimensional shape within the room to funnel into or cascade out of the roommate's mouth.

One morning, Mom explains, she saw the blankets on her hospital bed vibrating and shifting all around her. She asked her roommate if they were having an earthquake. The roommate said no. That's when the nurses moved her to a private room on a different hall, a children's ward. She was starting to frighten the other patients. They put her, for all intents and purposes, into solitary confinement.

"They moved me downstairs," she says, "and I remember pulling the sheet over my head. I was terrified. I didn't know what the hell was going on. The whole bed was vibrating, moving across and around the floor. My throat was so dry I couldn't talk."

She recalls that the room was long and narrow, her sense of perspective heightened. "You and your dad came to visit, and I saw you in the doorway. At first you were very, very small. Then you got closer and appeared very, very tall. I wanted you to leave. I didn't trust you, either of you."

At this memory, she stops. "You were both upset. But you, you looked so . . . I don't know. At least you were nice enough to leave me alone."

For the first time during this talk, I pause. I consider saying something. Or maybe asking for a sip of her beer. As I remember it, I wasn't being nice. I, too, had been terrified. I'd begun, throughout this crisis, to realize the weight of my mother's presence in my life in an incredibly tangible, physical way. Her rejections—even coming from an addled mind, even borne of her own fear and trauma and horrific luck with supposedly safe drugs—lodged in my body in a manner I can't describe.

When I say "can't," partially I mean "I've forgotten, on purpose." All the metaphors that come to mind are wrong because I have not lived them: watching death, giving birth, feeling a life ripped from my body. As a writer, I am disappointed in myself for having blocked the physicality of my hurt so completely that I cannot render it here, now. As a daughter, I think I am relieved.

~~~

When Thanksgiving came, Mom had only been home from this second trip to the hospital for a few days, her body still fragile but finally moving again after the drugs had cleared her system. But upon returning home, she'd quickly become constipated—a nuisance in any circumstance, but in my mother's state, a potentially life-threatening one.

Thanksgiving Day dawned unnaturally sunny and bright. Looking outside, I saw only one or two wisps of white interrupting the blue-sky canvas, the whole thing framed by rows of tidy, two-story, stucco homes on our suburban street. Mom suggested we take Buster for a walk.
~~~

"Maybe it'll help me fart," she'd said, shooting me an impish grin.

It was a relief to hear her being nice, cracking jokes—behaving a bit like her old self. My mother had always been one for a good fart joke. And she'd had a nurse in the hospital, Mauricio, who came to check on her every day and would always ask, "Did you fart yet?" We all loved Mauricio. But we also all knew now that her current condition made the act of farting something worthy of celebration.

The street formed one big circle, a perfect ten-minute loop. Every house along the way had been painted a different variation of the standard palette: pale beige, dark beige, beige pink, beige green. Here and there, neighbors were already mounting ladders to string Christmas lights above their garage doors and living-room windows. As we strolled, Mom and I smiled and waved, tugging Buster's leash as he stopped to sniff every hedge and mailbox. But before we'd even gone halfway, Mom slowed to a shuffle, said we needed to turn back.

At home, I settled Mom on the couch, then moved into the kitchen to start cooking dinner. She rested; I chopped and peeled. She moved to her bed; I preheated the oven. Her pain was getting worse, she said. But she refused to consider returning to the ER.

We should have called the doctor that afternoon, but we didn't. Instead, we busied ourselves with the business of waiting. My dad came home, changed clothes, and watched the football game. Evening came, and I put on a soft, stretchy purple wrap dress from Ross Dress for Less that I had purchased, pointlessly, several days earlier in preparation for this holiday dinner that, by now, I was almost certain none of us would eat.

By 6 p.m., the sky was dark. I could see the twinkle of candle-lit rooms from my bedroom window and hear laughter emanating from nearby patios and doorways. But our house was silent. My mother's pain had grown too distracting, too familiar for us to imagine away. Nausea swept over her, and soon she couldn't even leave the upstairs bathroom, the bathroom that was usually mine. I hovered. I didn't know what else to do.

We'd reached the point where she was either hunched up on the toilet or curled into a tiny ball on the towel-strewn floor.

"Call the doctor," she finally told my father, who promptly obeyed. Returning with vague instructions from the doctor's assistant for Mom to either "lie on her side or go to the ER," he then joined Buster and me in the bathroom doorway, where we stood, now hovering in concert.

At last, after vomiting a black, noxious, granular substance into the toilet, Mom gasped, "911." She clutched the bowl. Her face was white.

As Dad turned to fetch the phone, I heard her voice slip into a whisper.

"It's happening again . . . oh, God, it's happening again . . . I'm going to die this time."

The ambulance arrived. Three burly medics burst through the door and up the stairs, their bulky uniforms making them appear even bigger as they surrounded my mother, still curled around the toilet bowl on the floor. I stood by dumbly, Buster by my side, as the men maneuvered their way around the bathroom. They carried Mom downstairs. A rancid smell filled the hallway as they moved.

"Stay here with Buster," she managed to say to me.

"Yes," Dad echoed. "I'll follow the ambulance in my car." He reached over to give my shoulder a quick squeeze as Mom's head disappeared out of sight into the darkness. I jumped at his touch. Everything was happening too fast.

Standing on the front stoop, I watched Dad follow the medics across the yard to the driveway, their progress a strange parade of flashing lights and reflective tape and somber haste. Outside, the neighbors across the street had gathered to watch, their faces bathed in equal parts with curiosity and concern. One of the medics opened the back of the ambulance and a wave of light cut across the driveway, casting my mother's head in white gold, crowning her matted hair. First the fire truck, then the ambulance, and at last my father's BMW revved and roared, their headlights pouring fourth with a cacophony of yellow and red and piercing silver blue.

~~~

Sitting in my living room, Mom and I continue to rebuild the sequence of events. The sun shifts through the curtains. Lou rises, arching her back, slowly stretching one sharp-clawed foot and then the other out in front of her. I fight the urge to scratch the skin around my new tattoo as it begins to itch and flake. Mom sips her beer slowly. It is an IPA, not something she would order or choose—too bitter, too strong. It is all I have in the fridge.

As we talk, I can see, hear, even smell that Thanksgiving night they took Mom away. Hear my dad's voice through my flip phone as he explained that Mom was in a bubble, a plastic insulation blanket to keep her warm and boost her blood pressure. That the paramedics came close to losing her on the way to the ER. That her blood pressure had dropped dangerously low, and they had been unable to give her morphine because it would have killed her. But my memory blanks almost immediately after. Mom recalls that she was in the hospital for several weeks after the emergency rush to the ICU, feeling better before long but still failing to pass anything solid through her intestines. She and I begin to list the things she'd requested from home: books, cosmetics, a sound machine, an old CD Walkman. Scraps of memory begin to return to me. I type up our notes, everything she says, everything I've lost.

I'd completely forgotten what it was that finally helped Mom begin to recover until she starts to reminisce about the day she told her nurses about her active life before the surgery—Zumba, yoga, yardwork—and how hard it was for her now to move around as much as they wanted her to. In response, one nurse pursed her lips, then returned with a bag of yellow IV fluid.

"We usually reserve this for athletes," she said. "But let's give it a try."
~~~

My mother swears it took less than fifteen minutes for her to feel "reborn," the yellow blend (of proteins, electrolytes), sending her off wandering the halls, showing off her yoga stretches and legs-up-the-wall maneuvers in the visitors' room on the end of the wing. She felt better, but she wasn't healed. The healing took much longer and required a barium enema (this time, whatever drugs they gave her, an excellent trip, the kind where she saw "sea creatures" and "was in love with everyone afterward") and an experimental diet with some contraband deliveries—Marie Callender's custard pie, French fries, milkshakes, mashed potatoes—and, ultimately, one nurse's personal remedy: warm prune juice.

I remember the food. I remember the trip to Marie Callender's, a restaurant I had loved as a child in part because my mother had worked there in her early twenties and always told stories about those pies. I remember the McDonalds drive-thru for milkshakes and French fries. I remember the visits, sneaking in the treats; I was amenable to the secrecy so long as it was in custard pie or milkshake form, so long as it wasn't alcohol or drugs. I do not remember that the hospital chaplain had visited my mother, too.

I'd forgotten how Mom had told me afterward about their conversations: how she had spent those hospital weeks talking to me about her guts and her digestion and what she was reading and what she wanted to eat, but that she had talked to the chaplain—rightly so, and for once not to me—about her unhappy marriage. Her sense that my father was going through the motions when he came to visit, that he cared because he was supposed to and not because he truly did. That he loved her as the mother of his child and provided for her as his partner but did not love her body or her mind or her opinions. Her own warring yearning and disdain for him, in turns: the former something abstract and constant in her life, the latter specific to my father.

This, I am realizing, is not only the story of my mother's almost death. It is the story of a marriage death: the beginning of the ending, the new geometry of burdens and vows that would eventually take its place.

When she finally came home, my mother softened. She resolved, as she recalls it, to "change her attitude" and "foster affection" with my father. It was mid-December. She was so thin, finally well enough to do things, to get dressed. She attended Dad's office Christmas party in a black sequined skirt and silk blouse and black tights, feeling—in her words—as if she looked amazing (and it's true, she did), only realizing once they reached the party that her skirt was several sizes too big and at risk of slipping off entirely.

We had a Christmas I cannot remember. After that, a New Year. In the spring, A came to visit, a visit that became him moving in with us—that is, with me in my childhood bedroom, with my parents in the kitchen, living room, garage. This strange arrangement was, at least at first, a welcome novelty: my parents seemed to enjoy A's company, the four of us would go out to dinner, watch movies together and play with Buster in the yard. Having another person in the house put everyone on their best and most affectionate behavior.

Then the novelty and the post-healing haze began to lift. My father's attentiveness and, with it, my mother's sweetness, her determination, faded. Everyone got used to A's presence. Dad went back to his usual long days at the office and weekends reading the sports page on the recumbent bike in the garage or watching basketball on TV. Mom went back to drinking more frequently, earlier and earlier in the day. These cycles—my father's distance, my mother's alcohol abuse, the infinity loop of resentments that each behavior engendered in the other—tightened. The grooves wore deeper, harder. Dad, always tight-lipped and stiff in the arms; Mom, always blurring at the edges with her pain.

The truth is, everyone in the house was drinking more. Mom would go to bed early, and Dad and I would stay up with a bottle of wine, A usually joining us for a glass before taking a beer up to my bedroom and hiding out in my closet with his vaporizer, getting stoned and watching skydiving videos on his laptop. Dad and I would then have another glass, relax a bit, tell some jokes. I'd head upstairs eventually to find A in awe of the skydivers or listening to hip-hop on the closet floor, vapor seeping into the fabric of my dresses and coats, or already passed out across the bed. To each their own escape.

Then and now, it is hard to blame him. It is hard to blame any of us. Everyone was unhappy. Everyone felt trapped. A and I were trying to find jobs and make plans to move out, but jobs were scarce, as were my savings. I had good credentials, but no capital. A had savings, but an increasingly outdated résumé and degree. Meanwhile, Mom started coming home from her morning gym and yoga classes in full makeup and styled hair, her body perhaps the smallest it had ever been, with armfuls of flowers and Long Island iced tea on her breath, boasting about an apartment she'd seen for rent downtown.

"I just might move out," she'd say.

Dad, in front of the Warriors or Giants game, would remain silent. Make an infinitesimal downward motion with his head. Not so much a gesture of defeat as an acquiescence, a nod of agreement: *yes, please, one of us has got to go.*

Of course, the thing that went unsaid in all of this was money. My father was the only one who earned it, had it, had the agency to leave without an ask for help. Unless my mother got a job, the leaving would be up to him.

These last memories of my mother and father are my own. I jot them down after Mom leaves to run her Saturday errands, her bottle of beer still two-thirds full, abandoned in the sink. I consider finishing it, but the beer is warm. Instead, I pour the golden foam down the drain. Then I sit for a long time in front of this blank screen, this blinking cursor.

This story is hard because there is no ending. I mean, yes, there was an ending of sorts: the schism, the separation, then the divorce. But as for the rest of it—my mother and I, her health and my worry, her loneliness and my resentment—I'm realizing that there is only time. There is the epilogue of health concerns for my mother: more blockages, the carcinoma and the chemotherapy and hospice, the resultant perma-inflammation of her intestines that now makes digestive wellness a daily struggle. There is the continuation—and softening, perhaps—of shared trauma as we alike grow older, grow accustomed to our circumstances. Her health remains precarious. I remain her primary caregiver. There is very little chance that either of these facts will change. There is only what I can see more clearly now, at thirty-seven, looking back, looking forward: that at the time of my mother's severe health crises and my parents' final year of marriage, I hadn't known how to be at once relieved and angry, understanding and resentful. I hadn't figured out how to acknowledge and hold these contradictions inside myself. Perhaps my mother shared a parallel struggle. Perhaps she didn't know how to feel gratitude and anger, love and pain, how to manage the balance in her much-abused, still-tender body.

For most of my life, I've seen my mother as the central figure in our family equation, the high point of the triangle. Her moods, her emotions dictating the shape of our lives. She, I suspect, would say the opposite: that it was me in the center. Me, the child, taking hers and Dad's attention but also holding them together. That it had always been this way. That her surgery and resultant trauma had only superficially shifted the spotlight in her direction. I'm not sure my father would see us like a triangle at all. But when he left, removed that pin and the tension lines from our collective shape, the high point was gone. The angles flattened, became a direct and irrefutable line.

In 2010, I was in the first serious romantic relationship of my life. I was on the verge of moving away from my parents, this time to start a life of my own instead of simply leaving for college or a temporary, seasonal adventure. I felt entitled to this promise, this happiness. To a script that pronounced the coming years "my time," as if this were part of some binding contract, my payment for being a more or less "good daughter," obedient and respectful. But instead I felt what I can only describe as jealousy from my mother—not of my relationship with my partner, but of that promise our relationship represented. That I was young and permitted to leave, to start something new. That she was no longer young and had nowhere in particular to go. This jealousy was at once understandable and perverse. It felt dark and wrong, the way my resentment felt dark and wrong. It confused me, complicated my naïve sense of entitlement, and this in turn made me angry. The anger was likewise confusing in the wake of my mother's illness and trauma and, at last, her seeming physical recovery.

But I also understood. Somewhere, subconsciously, it all made sense. Mathematics, geometry. If my father and mother had chosen one another and now my father was unchoosing their marriage, the result left me in his place. If my mother held the triangle aloft and my father severed the tension in the ties, she and I were all that remained. His leaving shifted the balance of the equation: in exchange for his freedom, he deferred his vows to me.

It is now six years since I moved to Idaho for graduate school and five years since my mother followed me east—first several hours north of me in Coeur d'Alene, then down here to Moscow. It is also five years since A and I parted ways, first just physically when I left Los Angeles and, within the first year of my MFA, emotionally as well.

Now my mother lives alone on one side of this little town, and I live alone—that is, with Lou—on the other. For a long time, I resented this, too: her insistence on following me, staying nearby. I'd spent the better part of my teenage and adult life conflating my mother's proximity, her desire for intimacy in my day-to-day life, with the stifling of my own independence and freedom. Sometimes this was accurate. Many times, it was not.

Earlier this week, as I lay on the massage table in the tattoo parlor, as Karla carved the curvature and trident reach of a sagebrush stem along my forearm, I felt something shift inside. A kind of permission, perhaps: to remember the anger and the guilt without needing to feel it all again. To write it down rather than willfully forgetting. To ask my mother for her memories and stories rather than denying them out of fear—that they would hurt her, that they would hurt me.

I text Mom in the early evening to thank her for coming over. She tells me she is exhausted. Frankly, so am I.

"Sweet dreams, you girls," she writes. Lou and I, her girls. I tell her sweet dreams back, set my phone down, and move to the kitchen to make supper. After so much haze and smoke, it is a kind of wonder to rinse tomatoes, stem kale, with open windows and a mellow breeze.

BREACH

The night my father told me he was leaving was hot. High summer, and the air was still. Even with the windows open and the ceiling fan on, I struggled to breathe. Dad and I were sitting downstairs at the kitchen table, a bottle of Ménage à Trois red blend between us. It was—is—a cheap and accessible blend. Heavy, big with fruit. A bad choice in such weather. Assorted varietals of Ménage à Trois wines were frequently a mere eight bucks a bottle at Safeway. We stocked up in an effort to take the edge off our nightly conversations—conversations that, no matter where they'd started, always came back to him and Mom, to her mood swings, to his unhappiness. He bought the wine six bottles at a time.

"For the sale," he'd say. But we all knew better than that.

On this particular night, I sipped my wine and looked at Dad as he spoke.

"I just don't know what else to do," he said, after a long pause. "She's left me no choice."

I swallowed a big swallow, savoring the jam-sweet slick of the booze against my tongue.

"Is it permanent, do you think?"

He sighed, leaned back in his chair, held two long fingers against the base of his wine glass. "I thought about renting a place in the neighborhood, but it makes sense to be close to the office." With slow, circular movements, he swirled the wine. I watched his hands, paler than mine, streaked with fine dark hairs; watched the wine legs climb and dance towards the rim.

"I'm sorry," he said at last.

"It's okay," I replied, knowing I didn't mean it, not knowing how else to respond. "I mean, it's not 'okay'—but it's probably for the best."

"No matter what happens, I hope she and I can be friends."

"Of course," I said, my voice measured, diplomatic. "Me too."

I hadn't seen it coming. Not like this. I mean, I had seen their troubles. Watched the hurt and love worn thin between them. But I had always imagined a certain strength beneath the surface. Something cartilaginous, adaptable, like the tissue that surrounds the larynx, that permits us to breathe.

After Dad went to bed, I sat downstairs alone in the weighted warmth of the night and finished the wine. I thought about what would come next. Even in my twenties, it seemed shameful—the necessity, which would inevitably come, of telling people. I thought about the cruise my parents had taken to Alaska during the previous summer. How expensive it had been, and how unhappy they had seemed when they returned. I thought about how every phone call home, every visit, would have to be doubled.

I emptied the bottle. With the last sip, I tilted my head back. It coated my tongue with sugar and fog, and when it was gone, I closed my eyes and leaned my head against the granite countertop. I thought about the way Dad had asked me not to tell Mom yet, the way he had said he would handle it and not to worry. I thought about the worry that already lived inside of me. The worry that doubled and then doubled again as it hit: that once my father left, I'd be alone with my mother. No matter where I went, or how far I moved, she'd cleave to me; she'd follow.

~~~

Growing up, our family was always just the three of us: Mom and Dad and me. When things got tough, I was—I thought, anyway—the glue holding us together. I thought this was love. I thought we were happy. It wasn't until I was a little older, fourth grade, maybe fifth, that I consciously began to notice the resentment: on weeknights when Dad worked late and came home to find Mom drunk and mad, slamming pots and pans in the sink and then taking a bowl of spaghetti and a huge glass of pink wine upstairs to bed. I felt it on weekends when Mom came home from Zumba with stories about something she'd heard on NPR—about ancient Egypt, maybe, or how to prevent prostate cancer—only to have Dad blow her off because he was busy reading the sports page. (Whether he was, in fact, doing that or not, I no longer remember. I just remember it as Mom's refrain: "He'd rather read the sports page.")

When I was young, this toxicity hovered over us like a high cloud. Little by little it seeped into my air supply: first tickling my nostrils, then slipping down my throat.

It followed me to college. Every week or so, my mom would call me up.

"He wouldn't even notice," she'd say.

"Notice what?"

"If I left."

"Do you want to?"

There would be a long pause.

"Twenty years. Such a waste." I came to anticipate what came next. "Except for you. You were the reason we stayed together." She'd sniff, her voice coming back a little stronger. "If it hadn't
~~~

been for you . . ." She'd trail off. "I don't know. Sometimes I think you're the only reason I'm here."

What could I say? "Thank you"? "I'm sorry"? Usually, I'd come out with some version of both, make an excuse about a class or a homework assignment, say, "I love you," hurriedly, and then hang up. Back then, at least I could go outside afterward. Go for a walk, feel the icy northeastern wind slam against my skin. Tell myself that she and Dad would make up in the end, that I was allowed to be on my own, at last, across the country. Live my life. Make my own choices. Separate myself.

Sometimes, in Vermont, I could convince myself I was a free agent—utterly so—thanks to the combined magic of distance and snowfall and youthful ignorance, confidence. Even still, moments—phone calls—like this would catch against the space between my ribs.

~~~

"Take a deep breath."

It was spring 2008. I was twenty-three, newly returned from yoga camp, utterly in love with A and eager to practice everything I had learned during our month of training together on the beach. To teach—that is, rescue—everyone in my family. I was tan and taut and self-righteous. I was, in short, a total pain in the ass.

In this moment, my own ass was sitting perched on the edge of the sink in my parents' bedroom, and I was attempting to teach my dad how to do a few basic yoga poses. I was finding it a challenge.

Dad obeyed and inhaled through his mouth. I watched his shoulders rise, and with them his long arms, hands extended straight down, stiff. His chest and stomach rose in unison.

"You're breathing from the chest," I said. "Watch me." I inhaled, allowing my own belly to fill with air, feeling the fullness there first, low, then gradually high, and higher into my chest. Aware, as I did so, how much easier it is to extend the belly when there isn't much
~~~

there to begin with—when there's nothing to hide. I'd lost eight pounds in Baja, but gained muscle, and was now in exceptional shape, the best of my life. It was such a new, treasured experience, and a body for which my father and mother and others had given me such praise. Consciously, I carried myself with this knowledge. Unconsciously, I craved a stage to show it off: my body, its newfound discipline and strength.

I held the breath for a long moment, then exhaled loudly. "See how nothing moves? See how the breath starts at the bottom?"

Dad tried again. Exhaled quickly. Frowned. "That's hard." He looked at me, skeptical. "I thought deep breathing was supposed to feel good."

My dad is a lawyer. The type who can juggle reams of information about insurance litigation in his head and find that one detail, that single loophole, to win the case. He argues for a living, and when he gets home, he likes to relax. For my dad, that means watching the Giants on TV, taking a stroll downtown, eating at nice restaurants, cracking open a fancy cabernet. He has a talent for cheerfulness but gets brittle when he is hungry or under too much stress at work. Once a year or so, he cleans the garage. Twice a year or so, usually after a big trial, he gets sick and sleeps for two days straight. Off and on, he joins a gym, but seldom goes. His knees are bad. The timing is difficult.

"Try again, Dad," I said. "For now, if it hurts, that means you're doing it right."

He took another deep inhale. Air in, belly out. The whole time, his face and arms and neck and jaw were tense.

My yoga anatomy textbook explains that humans are built to breathe from the diaphragm, but few of us do. Most of us breathe instead from the chest, pulling up from the shoulders, cheating, using muscles and bones to support the shallow sips of air. We do this too much and the diaphragm gets lazy. The muscle atrophies, staying snug and comfortable up against the lungs, tucked above the stomach, hidden in the rafters of the ribs. The organs form a huddle that our breath doesn't touch.

Watching my father breathe was a textbook illustration in real time. How he pulled the air in, latched on with both sides of his body, yanked it up with his shoulders. He reminded me of a marionette. One that had gone stiff in the limbs, no longer free to amble and wave with the movement of its strings. I watched him and I thought about my mom. How she had once called him a "fucking robot." I watched him and I thought about his busy mind, his growing gut, his receding hairline; about the way he'd pushed me on the swings, taught me how to drive, watched *Gilmore Girls* with me every Tuesday night on the WB. (In our family, it was a father-daughter show—my mother hated what she called the "ridiculous, unrealistic" pace of the series' signature banter, but my father loved the wordplay.) How he still calls me Peanut.

Later, much later, I will feel this same restraint within my own body: a tightness, a forward motion of the shoulders, a rounding of the lower belly, a weakness of the abdomen and back. I will, due to the resurgence of a global pandemic thanks to a predatory variant, be instructed to wear a face covering at the gym and find myself constantly short of breath as I walk or jog or spin the footbeds of the elliptical machine, my breath trapped, urgent and rapid and stuck above my heart. I will give up easily: quit spinning, jogging, walking. I will use the weight machines to save face, to ensure I'm there for the thirty-minute minimum I assign myself once I make the drive to the rec. And then I will leave because it is hard, this breathing, this actual oxygenation thing our bodies require us to do and do correctly. It is hard and I will find myself, in this moment, struggling in many ways.

I am nothing if not self-critical. But for a few blissful months, in 2008, at twenty-three, I was just young enough and newly in love enough and thin enough and toned enough to believe in the version of myself my yoga teacher training and resultant love-affair-turned-boyfriend had made visible: a strong self, benevolent and correct. Someone who knew the power of her body and how to foster that power in others. It was a fleeting power, one I would revisit several times again throughout my twenties, each iteration flagging in its brilliance, its certainty. But in that moment, in that bathroom with my father and my ego and my still-tanned arms and curlicue legs, all I knew was how to proselytize and demonstrate. Me, a peacock prophet in my emerald-green yoga pants and tie-dye tank tops; my father slowly but surely filling out around the middle.

I thought I was helping. Looking back, I wish I'd just spent time with Dad watching *Gilmore* reruns and laughing together.

~~~

When I was a kid, I struggled to catch my breath. It wasn't asthma, or a lack of fitness. Just a heaviness in my chest that made me feel the need to yawn. I called it "the breathing thing": one inhalation after another getting thinner, failing to satisfy. It always struck in times of high anxiety, like a calculus test or a fight with my mother, or when I was unable to fall asleep the night before an early morning flight. In its grip, I would get light-headed and panicky, easily exhausted but restless.

I wouldn't learn the physiology behind "the breathing thing" until I turned twenty-six, the year after my parents would ultimately split. This would be the year my mother would all but threaten to kill herself; the year my dad would confirm he was done, that he was never coming back; the year Mom would announce she couldn't stand to live in our house anymore, pack up the Prius and drive south to Chino to stay with her cousin; the year she would suffer yet another intestinal blockage and have to have yet another emergency surgery, this time in an unfamiliar hospital with an unfamiliar surgeon. It would be the year both she and my father would play me like a game of Telephone, passing messages back and forth because they wouldn't speak to one another. It would be
~~~

the year—or, rather, the first year—I would begin drinking far too much, breathing too little, crying too often, panicking while driving down a steep hill and waking up in the night afraid I had a blood clot or a heart arrhythmia or some weird and sudden form of cancer.

Throughout that year, I would get up and get dressed and put on makeup and go to my new job as a copywriter at a local marketing company. I would chat with my boss and eat my lunch salads and handle my clients' phone calls and emails and smile at meetings. After work, I would come home, and often A and I would get dinner at some kind of happy-hour place (the options were plentiful in Ocean Beach) so we could eat and drink for cheap. Tacos and beers and heavy pours of house white wine at the Blue Parrot, or sliders and beers and heavy pours of house white wine at the Arizona Grill. Throughout that year, we would stop at the liquor store on our short walk back home to grab a six-pack, maybe a bottle of Barefoot pinot grigio, before curling up on the couch to watch TV.

Through all of this, I would imagine I felt just fine. It would be the breathing thing, the driving fear, the midnight worries that would eventually make it clear that something was wrong.

This would be the year when I'd wake one night with a cramp in my calf. A gripping, seizing kind of pain, as leg cramps often are. Unpleasant but nothing all that unusual—except that it wouldn't resolve with the usual stretching or massage. In a half-sleep haze punctured now with rising panic, I would stand up fast and walk to the bathroom to deepen the stretch, to move my muscles. The pain would worsen, tighten, and with it so would my fear. I wouldn't remember what came next, but A would later tell me I'd passed out in the doorway of our bedroom—my first and only proper faint. He'd crouched down to hold me there, crumpled on the carpet, until I came to. Because I'd never fainted before, never had what I now believe was a panic attack and couldn't recognize my symptoms, we would go to the ER. I would, in my anxiety, be positive something was very seriously wrong with me. They would run all the tests, check my heart, find nothing. Eventually, I would be sent home with several blurry, overly Xeroxed pages instructing me to stretch my legs.

Medical analysis, in other words, would prove to be unconvincing. I would begin seeking other avenues for support. That spring, I would go to see an integrative massage therapist (as well as his wife, the holistic nutritionist I'd later push on my mother) whom I'd met at my yoga studio. The therapist's name would be Hugo, and he would be skinny with a black goatee, earrings made of bone, a topknot streaked with gray. In a less vulnerable state, I would have been skeptical of a man like this. But he would have a kind, toothy smile and a peaceful energy that put me at ease, and, in this particular year, I would crave ease above everything else.

Hugo would put his hands on my upper back and feel my breath through my bones. He would explain that the first and most immediate trouble had to do with my breath. That it was not about breathing in, but about the letting go afterward: voiding the lungs, releasing the diaphragm, letting it rise all the way to my ribs. When I got home, I would try his advice: breathing out, pushing the diaphragm up, pushing until I couldn't push anymore. But something inside me would not budge.

~~~

In the womb, babies breathe through their mothers. The first infant breath is the breaking apart. It inflates the alveoli, tiny air sacs in the lungs where oxygen and carbon dioxide trade places. It opens the baby's lungs like balloons, lifting the child from the deep well of mother love and into the world. The first breath is a breach.

When I was born, my first breath was ripped from my lungs through a tube shoved down my trachea. I was two weeks late. Everything was running behind schedule. The doctors feared I would inhale my own feces, so they yanked the breath up and out of me with a laryngoscope as I arrived, red-faced and angry.

Looking at my mother, I wonder what her first breath was like.
~~~

I wonder how it felt to breathe for us both. "You can't possibly know," she says, "until you have a kid of your own." I tell her I'm sure she is right; that I can't imagine. But then I think of all the times I've lain awake worrying: if she is okay, if she is sober enough to drive home, if she took too many Ativan or Vicodin or Ambien or simply didn't bother to count. If, unable to sleep at 3 a.m., she is writing another angry email to my father. If her insides are twisted and cramping and closing in on themselves yet again.

I think about what it means to be responsible for someone else's life. And I wonder about my own first breath: if there is still something left of it, buried inside of me.

~~~

After the separation and her subsequent move to Chino, my mother and I visit often. We email or talk on the phone most days of the week. Usually, our conversations are little more than rambling thoughts, spoken aloud. But sometimes things stick. Like once, she told me that she holds her breath for long minutes at a time. Not on purpose, but out of unconscious habit, the way others might chew pencils or tap their feet. Ever since that conversation, whenever we are together, I watch her: washing dishes after we've made dinner, her hands scrubbing fast under hot water. Or staring off into space in the morning as she listens to her Bible study podcasts, face still, eyes glassy and unmoving. I see her thoughts turn back, see how long it takes for her to find the space, the break in her reverie, for a breath. I listen as she frees the thick air. I imagine it as cloudy inside. She lets go in weak little puffs, and the stillness makes me notice how time and sadness have made a hillside of her shoulders, round against her neck.

Time passes. We reach the four-year mark of my father's leaving. When Dad comes up in conversation, Mom vacillates between anger, sadness, curiosity, and pity. I do my best to avoid the subject. But sooner or later she always pulls him into the space between us.
~~~

By the summer of 2014, A and I have moved from San Diego to Los Angeles. We're closer to my mom this way, among other things—a comfort, after the cancer treatment and subsequent hospice, knowing we're nearby if she needs anything. A has decided he wants to try acting. I'm doing freelance work, ghostwriting, and waiting tables at a trendy Taiwanese restaurant. My career, such as it is, isn't glamorous, but being in Los Angeles makes it easy to pretend.

One July morning, Mom picks me up in Silver Lake. We eat lunch, then climb back into her Prius for the return drive to Chino, where I'll stay for a few nights. A "girls' weekend." In the car, we chat lightly about the heat, the traffic. Then Mom stops talking to slide into the carpool lane, and we settle into an easy seventy-miles-per-hour groove. I'm looking out the window, watching the signs coast by: Figueroa, Verdugo, Colorado.

Her voice interrupts:

"I know you don't want to talk about it. But . . . does your father ever ask about me?"

She poses this question, on average, once or twice a month. Always with the same apologetic preface, always with the same plaintive voice that sends a shot of tension through my chest.

"He asks how you're doing every time we talk, Mom. I've told you this before."

I wait, expecting questions, accusations—all of the words she wants to say to Dad but can't anymore outside of the occasional drunken email, that she says to me instead, that she has said to me repeatedly since he moved out. I wait for her to tell me that he is a passive-aggressive fuck, that it's his fault she couldn't quit drinking, that he is incapable of change, that he is brittle and unloving. But she is silent, and when I look over, I see that there are tears in her eyes. Her face turns red, screwed up like a prune. Then a tiny sob forces its way through, and something cracks.

~~~
~~~

That summer night with Dad in the kitchen stretches through memory. No doubt, it warps. I do my best to remember it faithfully, but I also know this is impossible. If I honor memory alone, if I trust it, I permit the night to stretch on indefinitely. A string of sensations and colors and temperatures, recalled on repeat.

In this scene: I open a second bottle of wine and take it with me into the living room. Digging out our old family photo albums, I look at pictures of the two of them. Pictures of Dad's arm around Mom, their smiles wide and artificial. I look at pictures of the three of us—out to dinner at the cheap strip-mall sushi place they loved when I was a toddler, the place where our waitress gave me a deluxe marker set for Christmas and taught me how to use chopsticks, tethering the two blonde strips of wood together with thin pink rubber bands. Or the three of us, riding the San Francisco Bay ferry: me dressed in my father's too-big puffy vest and clutching a Teenage Mutant Ninja Turtle I'd won at Pier 39. I remember the way my dad's oversized glasses reflected too much light, leaving his eyes blurred. I remember my mother's hair, long and wild and curly in the wind. I remember us three riding up near the front of the boat, standing outside, letting the bay breeze whip us silly.

In this scene, I am turning the album pages, gulping air into my mouth again and again and holding it there.

~~~

Mom and I spend the rest of that drive to Chino in relative silence. Once, I reach over and rest my hand lightly on her knee, just for a minute or two. This gesture feels at once necessary and invasive—too intimate, perhaps, but who else will do it? I wait for a respectful period, then gently shift my hand back to my own lap. Mom tunes in to NPR. Traffic is light.

When we get to her house, we set about making supper, chopping beets in her kitchen. Her tears have subsided and, with them, some of her anger. She's lapsed into one of her rare nostalgic moods,
~~~

telling me about the first few years of her marriage to my father. How surprised she had been when he gave her the real diamond engagement ring at Dante's in San Francisco. (She'd been sure it was fake.) How pleasant the idea of a nice man with a steady job had seemed at the time after a string of flashy, difficult men she couldn't count on. I've heard these stories before. More recently—as things with A got increasingly serious, our lives increasingly enmeshed, as he persisted in flitting from one unpaid hobby or student film or improv class to the next without having yet held down a job since Tahoe, as my interest in writing grew quietly, increasingly ambitious and my wondering about our shared future together louder and louder in my subconscious—they'd begun to sound all too familiar. For various reasons, even her good memories leave a mixed taste in my mouth.

"We were married for two years before you were born," she says. "I had some doubts then, but it wasn't until you were about one and a half that we both realized we'd made a mistake."

She wrestles with a slippery roasted beet, peeled and still hot. Pinning it down on the cutting board with one hand, she holds her knife inexpertly against its flesh with the other.

I pause, startled. *Mistake*?

"We talked about splitting up," she says. "And who knows? Maybe I should have gone through with it then." She keeps chopping, awkwardly. "But I was too scared. Of being a single mother, of being alone. And your father . . ." Here she pauses, tilting her head to the right. Softening just the slightest bit. "Your father wasn't willing to see you only every other weekend. He wanted to be part of your life." She shrugs. "I guess I have to give him that. It gave me hope that things would change."

Wait a minute. I don't say this, but I want to. My mind slows down, struggling to assimilate what I've just heard. I feel the usual guilt, at first, and then for the first time, a surge of something much more like relief.

It is in this moment—with Mom, with the beets and the knife

and the heat of the sun outside beating hard at the windows—that I first recognize, understand, if only for an instant, that maybe her unhappiness isn't my fault. That if what she's said is true, then perhaps I don't have so much to mourn. That perhaps what was lost was not so much a happy family, but the hope for one, someday, to bloom. Still a tragedy, but one long understood by the responsible parties involved. It dawns on me that this new version of the story might free me from the mire of "what might have been." What happiness they might have ultimately found if they had stuck it out; stayed together. What might have been different if only I had found some magic way, as I had always thought myself capable as a child, to keep the glue from flaking.

I let out a sigh—a big one, puffing my lips, blowing the air out hard. I push until my chest feels empty. The sigh is a purge. It leaves me feeling lighter, like something stale has left my body. Then I look up and see that my mother has been watching me. Her face is shadowed with concern.

"Should I not be telling you this?"

I pick up her knife and take over, slicing halved beets into smooth quarters.

"No. It's good, actually. Thank you. I'm glad to know all that."

She looks dubious, but nods. I watch as she resumes her work, moving on now to the celery. I think about the fear—the fear and the hope—that made her stay married. That made my childhood what it was, my adulthood and my own romantic partnership what it has been.

I reach out and touch her shoulder.

"Okay. So, now: where do you want these beets, Mom? Where do we go from here?"

ENCAUSTIC

I never meant to keep them. Hard stubs stuck inside the guts of cups or crusted flush against the cheap aluminum of tealight tins. A rim of wax, a blackened wick. The scent still held, like perfume lingering along my wrist.

It is my first early Idaho spring. I'm newly thirty-one, finishing my first full year of graduate school. The weather refuses to turn, the skies threaten rain almost daily, but the trees are budding—just at the tips, little green points waving from gray branches. My apartment has stopped feeling new and started to feel like it is mine. I've grown accustomed, after nearly eight years of cohabitation, to living on my own.

Last week, the moon was full. Ever since, I've been feeling restless, tense. Feeling a stirring of something that keeps me up too late, keeps me awake, makes me take hot showers, finds me talking to myself, the words lulled out of me beneath the heat and wet, the rhythmic pulse of water.

Sometimes I imagine conversations with A, who is back in Los Angeles. Other times I imagine conversations with the poet, who lives around the corner. Neither imagining soothes.

I've never been one for a circumscribed bout of spring cleaning. But lately, in the daylight, in the twilight, I get the urge to root through things—junk drawers, closets, notebooks. I feel the need to purge. That's how I find them, hiding in the cupboard. Odd-sized holes, these apartment cupboards; awkward spots where nothing normal fits.

I stand on my toes, grope around, take things down. On the righthand side: old sponges, paper towels, bottled veggie wash, Seventh Generation counter cleaner. On the left: one twenty-four-count box of tealights bought at Ross, two packs of unscented pillars marked "EMERGENCY," three brass candlesticks of varying heights, one black kickstand flashlight. Then my fingers wander all the way into the back, all the way into the deep and dark, and I discover them. Candle shells, fallen votives, smudged-up jars with price tags still affixed. I strain my neck to look and find a crypt. A graveyard full of wax.

In nature, wax is a secretion: sticky, yellow, moldable stuff, made by bees to build a hive. In industry or chemistry, it is "a viscous substance," variably derived from tallow, soy, petroleum, or palm. In art, it can be blended with pigment, heated, and applied to a canvas to create moldable, sculptural forms. Of the moon, it means to light a larger swath of surface, pulsing out at us from cloaked new moon to full. In poetry, "to wax" is to grow bigger, stronger—or else, to write, to speak (as in, "he waxed lyrical about her eyes, her cheeks, her lips"). The oldest versions of the word stem from Latin, from the root *augere*: "to increase."

Somehow, then, I've managed to collect that which collects. To hoard the stuff of growth in this, my newfound solitude.

But this is not the kind of growth I want. It feels like a haunting.

~~~

As a child, I feared fire most of all. So much more than other things—spiders, monsters, ghosts. I practiced for fire: popping out the bedroom window screen, imagining sliding down the eave,
~~~

gripping gutters tight, then lowering myself to the gravel. This was my escape route. I was nine years old, and paranoid. I had concerns. I made contingency plans. After all, the drop from gutter to gravel was a good eight feet, and I was tall for my age but not that tall. I considered asking my parents for a ladder.

We lived in the new house then. Bloated, beige, suburban. Ostensibly an upgrade. This was 1994: Bill Clinton and the boom and steadily rising GDP. This was the year we left the little duplex I'd loved as a child and graduated up the hill to Southampton, a development of multistory, cookie-cutter, nineties pastel homes. It was the year I got a Littlest Pet Shop for my birthday—as in, the shop itself, not just the pets—and my father leased a wine-red Jaguar, and my mother went a brighter shade of blond; the year of puffed-up poofed-up *stuffness*—stuff to fill this space we didn't need. The double doors and vaulted eaves and three-car garage and stucco, stucco everything. Cabinets and refrigerators jammed full of nonfat diet replacements for the realness of sugar, fat: Smart Ones, Jenny Craig, I Can't Believe It's Not Butter. And a fireplace we didn't use for actual fire, but instead for a candelabra my mom filled with sickly sweet vanilla-scented pillars.

My mother was always on a diet in those days. Lite mayo, nonfat milk, nonfat cottage cheese. This was all we had in the kitchen, so, in essence, I was always on a diet, too. Always eating leaner substitutes for the real thing, the sweetness, richness that I craved. Nevertheless, our home smelled perpetually of fake sugar. This was before my mother would learn to worry over artificial scent and smoke. Instead, back then, she worried over dirt: the coal and soot. She said it was unhealthy.

~~~

I'm reading about candle lore and rituals and spells online to unlock my subconscious. To understand my strange collection: all these little waxen bodies shoved away and out of sight. I draw
~~~

up many lists. The internet insists that red candles in a dream mean sex, and white ones equal marriage, and green ones equal money; that how a candle burns and cracks and melts reveal "spirit whispers."

This sounds silly to me at first. But then I think about the way my expensive Gold Coast candle pops and spits each time I light it up—the candle I brought from home, from California—and of everything and everyone I've left behind. I think of its notes of scent: ocean spray and eucalyptus, white lavender and redwood. I think of all the love I once felt there; of all the plans to move back to Los Angeles, to keep returning each summer and winter holiday; of the warm summer night before I moved away, when A and I drank too much bourbon and sat on our brand-new white flokati rug—the rug we'd bought together with money from our joint account, an account he filled with transfers from his dwindling savings and I filled with my meager paychecks from the hipster restaurant where I worked—and dreamt up the whole thing: a wedding in Ojai, cacti in mason jars, my vintage crocheted dress, his scribbled outline of a custom ring.

The money, the receipts, the life that came next . . . we didn't talk about that then.

I think of how happy and excited and tipsy we were that night. How I'd treasured up that ring sketch (even if I couldn't quite decipher what A had pictured, rendered in an abstract, shaky scrawl on that paper scrap), tucked it inside a notebook. How A's enthusiasm for a wedding had vanished with the dawn. How, over time and distance, my disappointment turned first to resignation, then relief.

I watch the flame rise way too high, too fast, and how it smokes.

~~~

Candles are contrary bodies. Seductive and inconstant. A performance, a mood, a safer cousin of the cigarette. Like candles, cigarettes offer scent and warmth—but with the latter there is also
~~~

touch and taste. The noirish beauty of a glowing cigarette tip, so close to the mouth. How it looks to let a curl of smoke drift gently from between the lips.

I imagine myself with an unlit cigarette like Lauren Bacall in *To Have and Have Not*, her voice full, deep, and low; how, only just nineteen years old, she undoes a salty Bogart twice her age, all business in her houndstooth tweed. Her voice a throaty purr, asking Bogart for a match.

But the truth is, I do not smoke, and I still hate matches. The risk. The way a lit match heats my fingertips. The way I'm forced to strike it quickly, with force, or not at all. No room for *wait and see*. Nothing like the understated, almost androgynous sex of Bacall's slight waist and shoulder pads offset by rich dark lips and subtle waves of curl against her cheek. The way she lets the cigarette rest, her mouth barely open, her eyes enveloping Bogart. The way he watches her, his gaze up and down her suited body, her soft hair, in those seconds before she strikes a flame.

~~~

After cleaning my apartment, I take inventory:

Two burnt-down tealights, aluminum
Two burnt-down tealights, plastic
One burnt-down travel candle, scented, pumpkin spice
One burnt-down sanctuary candle, plain white, unscented
One burnt-down emergency candle, plain white, unscented
One burnt-down beeswax aromatherapy candle, palmarosa and lavender, for "Sensuality"
One burnt-down chakra candle, Moroccan rose and chamomile, for "Positive Energy"
One burnt-down chakra candle, lavender and chamomile and fir, for "Abundance"
~~~

Of these ten, seven I simply found: candle corpses dug out from the cupboard. The other three I burn on purpose, waiting to see what will happen, what they might say. I light them on a Friday night after dark, after drinks down the road at the wine bar with the poet.

The poet and I spend too much time together—making dinner, buying groceries, trading books, grading papers, sipping wine, walking to and from the bar at night to meet our other grad-school friends downtown. Underneath it all, I know I am betraying A by continuing this way. That it is a kind of emotional infidelity to eat pasta over candlelight at the poet's apartment, listening to his records, and telling him private things about my partner, about our faltering relationship, about my doubts. I'm sure the poet knows it, too. But we do not stop. Instead, we grow closer. He tells me about his ex, his heartbreak. I meet his parents when they come to town and we go to dinner, just the four of us. When the poet keeps appearing in my dreams, I am at once excited and afraid.

Though I refuse to admit it to anyone, I want him to make a move. To close the increasingly narrow gap between our intimate conversations, our domestic behaviors, our blazer-clad bodies. To disarm me beyond the point of resistance. And sometimes, on nights like that dark night at the wine bar, it seems inevitable. The way our bodies lean close to one another at the low-lit bar, the tealights flickering, the flames reflecting off the open bottles on the counter.

I want the tension to break because it is so high between us. I assume, in wanting this, that I also want the poet. But I am not certain. What would I do in response if this man beside me let his touch linger on my shoulder, let it warm the lonely skin along my collarbone, my neck, soften my resistance with its heat. Do I simply want to know that he desires me? Do I, in fact, desire him? Or do I merely want some reassurance—from him, from anyone—that I am still desirable?

At home, I light the candles in a row—one, two, three—and set them on a platter by my desk. Here is how they burned:

"Abundance" glowed steadily, even and slow, with little flicker. The label explains that this votive's color and aroma represent one's psychic powers. It reads, "Your true self will attract unlimited resources, power, and compassion to realize your destiny."

"Sensuality" burned steadily, too—much more than I'd expected, to be honest, though with greater thinning and cracking around the top as it sank, concave, into a molten pool of its own making.

"Positive Energy" was the wild card: sputtering, then melting slantwise, the pale blue wax collapsing to the right and rippling around its base. The label explains that the candle's color and aroma represent the throat chakra, one's "center of communication." It reads, "You will be drawn to meet new and wonderful people and embrace experiences that will encourage your spiritual growth."

A website tells me that steady-burning candles portend victory. Or something like it, I suppose. The site suggests that a strong burn signals "a green light," that "your intent is clear, and your prayer or spell has been successfully sent." A sideways burn, however—one that droops and slants—warns of incompleteness. An "unresolved or unsettled" situation. The site notes that, in the face of such a burn, one should "refocus your intention, find a better candle, try again."

It is a ridiculous solution—to simply light another candle. Like shaking a Magic 8 Ball until you get the answer you want. But of course, this is precisely what I am doing. Later, I will realize that I was too afraid to search myself for the truth of my own feelings. To acknowledge that my life was changing, that I was changing—or maybe reintegrating a long-buried part of myself, an essential part, here in this town, with these writers and teachers and students and ideas—and that things with A had not been perfect, or healthy, for some time. That we might not be right for one another after all. That I loved A, imagined that I always would, imagined we would always feel like soulmates of a kind . . . but didn't want a life held tightly to his life anymore.

But in the moment, sitting here, watching my candles burn, I don't know this yet—not clearly, anyway. I only know I feel increasingly inclined to stay in Idaho over the summer. That the last time I'd been back to visit A my body seemed to hold and hold and hold: everything I ate, drank, touched turned heavy, thick, inside. That the heaviness evaporated within days of returning to the snow and cold of Idaho, that it turned to lightness and ease when I was once again alone.

~~~

When my parents separated, they ditched the stucco house and leased it out. The stuff, though, they kept. Stacked plastic tubs from Target packed with sixteen years' worth of toys, tax write-offs and talismans. This was 2011: Barack Obama, recession slump, employment gaps, precarity. This was the year that I moved out for the third time, stashing trunks of clothes and books and CDs and "save-forever" boxes in the three-car garage before driving south to San Diego. My parents found a tenant who didn't mind the furniture, the cluttered garage—a tenant who wouldn't, in other words, force them to reckon with the orphaned objects of their ended marriage. They left it there—all of it, the stuff, mine and theirs—until last month, when finally, the house went onto the market and they began, without me there, to sort it all.

I started getting text messages from my mother every day: "Do you want the old armoire? Your dress-up clothes? This box of trophies? What about the American Girl doll? Your yearbooks, sand toys, puzzles?" A part of me felt pangs each time I heard the ringer buzz, each time I saw the screen filled up with text. There
~~~

were so many stories, memories, imbued in those things. Love, nostalgia, regret. But stronger than all that was the need to move on, to lose dead weight—and it emboldened me. I wanted none of it. Suddenly, vehemently, violently. I wanted nothing of the past, that house, its memories.

"Donate everything," I texted back.

~~~

For several days, the moon persists in its brightness. Electric in the night sky as I lay in bed, unable to sleep. Its body waxed and bursting like the flowers on my street—flowers suddenly explosive in their crimson-pink fecundity.

I've never seen such unabashed flora, such flagrant sex daring to show off against the prosy sidewalk gray, damp with April rain. One moment, all is tight-budded tension: the dahlias a red orb pushing against a petal casing. Then the sun hits just right and petals kaleidoscope outward. A sculpture, stunning and evanescent. The flower's form, once sprung, beholden to the heat.
~~~

INTERLUDE: SALT

2018

My body is tall and soft. Filled with lemons, radishes, and figs. Round and wanting shapes, voracious in their thirst.

I am not a gardener. My houseplants rarely live. I overwater, then neglect.

The lover I loved longest used to call me a camel. He said I stored sex like water in my blood.

He was wrong. With lack comes madness.

I reach for anything I see that's cool and liquid, brimming in a glass.

I think back to the hands that knew my body once, the lips, the lines they marked and traced along my skin: neck to collarbone to breast. Their desire and my need combined to render clumsy maps: hesitant fingers, an amateurish tongue. Other times, touch that fell with shivering exactitude. How a man can know precisely where to place his hands.

My first summer alone, I dizzied; dry mouth damp for anything I thought I could have.

Last week, a student in my class complained, "This author only describes all the ways other women are doing feminism wrong. *How are we supposed to do it right?"*

How, indeed. How to want the things we should.

Reserves of anything—water, wanting, sex—diminish over time.

In summer, my leather lace-up sandals leave pink marks along my ankles. I worry over salt: how much I've consumed. My body, greedy for scant water. Where to find enough.

DISTANCE INSTRUCTIONS

Sunday afternoon. Spring lifting her skirt, sky-blue, and a mellow warmth against my neck. I walk to the middle school track and run a mile in a t-shirt, cushioned knees on polyurethane. I don't need to use my hands, but the moment I arrive back home, I wash them anyway.

"Distance learning" is the recommended phrase. "Online classes" aren't enough for students from abroad who need to keep their visas. Semantics of the pandemic, like "social distancing" and "flatten the curve."

This morning it is gray. Windy. Classes begin at nine.

Texting with my friend Kristin, I try to explain the singular discomfort I feel when video conferencing with my male undergraduate students via Zoom. Here is the difference: video makes me feel like I need to look polished, put-together, piped into these young men's kitchens and childhood bedrooms. I've yet to hold a video conference with a female student; my suspicion is that this will come with equal self-consciousness but easier intimacy.

Something akin to the group chat with college girlfriends, my former Suite I roommates, I participated in on Sunday night. Our first in nearly five years.

Audio, on the other hand—which some have said is best for equitable distance instruction as it requires much less bandwidth—makes me feel both comfortable and powerful. The focus is my voice, my words. Not my appearance. I can look wherever I need to as I'm thinking, eyes darting left and right, hair askew, glasses finger-smudged. The ubiquitous leggings.

~~~

Today I slept in, then stayed in bed an extra hour with a headache, general malaise. Finally awoke to the radio, boiling water, the public broadcasting host talking to truckers and farmers and food distributors about the very real chance of running out of supplies, the Herculean efforts required to repackage restaurant products for individual consumers.

I made sprouted toast with just a hint of butter, fried an egg. Coffee. The meal felt decadent even though I eat it nearly every day.

My particular brand of clinical anxiety manifests as a vertiginous sensation, a kind of flutter inside my brain and around my eyes. Not dizziness so much as a subtle, clouded, drifting feeling—like the first few seconds of a marijuana high before it really floods the system. This might sound pleasurable, but it isn't because I do not get to choose when it will strike (usually in the morning). It stifles my breathing, makes focusing on words and screens and typing difficult. Eating helps. Grounds me in my body, in the literal weight and material substance I am taking in. Pocket stones.

Thanks to Jia Tolentino's essay collection, *Trick Mirror*, and my forced reckoning with the critical attitude I often turn toward my body, now that my body and I are so much alone together, I've been thinking a lot lately about self-optimization. The sense I felt, almost immediately, when faced with the prospect of quarantine:
~~~

make the most of this time, be productive, lose five pounds, tone your arms; don't waste the opportunity to self-improve.

In her essay "Always Be Optimizing," Tolentino digs between the tricky cracks, the patterned loops, that fail to separate feminine empowerment via beauty, strength, and self-care from the deeply patriarchal industry of selling women stuff to cure (read: reinforce) their feelings of inadequacy—and/or selling women stuff that enhances their sexual capital.

It is at once very easy to see and very difficult to extricate myself from this web.

I sent a truncated version of the essay, published in *The Guardian*, to my college friends after a Saturday evening virtual happy hour on Zoom that lasted for nearly four hours. My former roommate wrote back: "I liked the article you sent, but I wish it had more actionable next steps."

Of course, this is the difference between a self-help article and a personal essay. Between the truncated version and the whole unwieldy thing. By the end of "Always Be Optimizing," it seems clear to me—and, I think, to Tolentino—that the awareness born of writing through and between the impulse to optimize does not lead to a so-called solution. The lines between health and self-care, between power and adherence to the patriarchy, between self-defined beauty and that which the media and Instagram influencers would have us long for, strive for . . . perhaps especially for those of us raised with the internet always buzzing in the background or foreground of our lives, with mothers always on a diet, with fathers who left for or eventually ended up with younger women, with boyfriends who left for or eventually ended up with younger women, with just enough or more than enough privilege to taste the power that comes with adherence or at least aspiration to the ideal—these lines are not only fused, they are inextricable from our identity codes. Removal would require major surgery. Considerable remaking of the self.

And after? Isolation.

After all of this: how will we unmake and remake ourselves?

I want the question and the answers to provide a source of light. Of hope. But many of the answers come with more criticism, judgment, aspiration—both necessary and not, depending on the "we" in question.

Sarah and I, texting this afternoon.

"I feel like maybe everything means a new thing?" she writes.

"It is very self-evaporating, this situation," I write back.

~~~

Trying to find grounding in one's personal goals seems pointless, multiple times each day. Writing is the only thing that feels productive. Writing, and walking. Moving forward, bodies and text. The only way to advance with no need for an answer, an endpoint.

This morning, I read the news in bed, on my phone, then skimmed through Instagram ads for at-home workout programs. Open the fridge, find that I've consumed two-thirds of a jar of almond butter in about three days.

What else is there at night, in the dark, anticipating nearly 10,000 new cases every day? Almond butter. Wine. Uncooked sweetened oatmeal packets, consumed straight from the bag with a spoon. My tongue in the paper crevices, looking for that last trove of sweet salt buried in the corner.

~~~

More than 3 million people filed for unemployment last week. Last night, Congress passed a $2 trillion aid bill. It feels as though I'm living a split existence: the one where things will soon be normal and $1,200 in the mail is something to look forward to, just like the clearance summer slacks I bought online last week as consolation for my homebound existence; the other, where this goes on for months, where friends and neighbors fall gravely ill or even die, where restaurants shutter and my summer arts class is canceled and writing is only for myself because the publishing industry shuts down, my teaching job hangs in the balance, students can't come back to campus.

Both seem possible and impossible this morning.

I want to take a long walk, buy a bottle of scotch. I want to curl into a ball and stay inside and slug coconut cream from the can. Suck down fat as ballast for this drifting self, affixed to static body. Every few days, despite not having left the house or seen another person from closer than six feet since Sunday, I get the urge to disinfect every surface in my house. Do laundry, except that the machines in my apartment complex are communal and disgusting even in non-pandemic times.

Last night I slept heavily. Today I've gained a pound. Perhaps it is worth it to feel weighted down in sleep.

~~~

Outside, a nearly invisible snow drifts past the pines. Inside, the forced hot air pops on intermittently to keep the apartment somewhere in the realm of sixty degrees. The *Friday News Roundup* on NPR is at once predictable and horrific: record deaths in Italy and Spain, Japan's decision to postpone the 2020 summer Olympics. I don't feel well. Weighted belly, tight abdomen. My breath feels trapped someplace behind my ribs. I leave the office lights off. Type this in the mellow dark.

Stagnant body starts to move. Begins with the fingers. Caffeine travels through my brain like wire.

All I want to eat is steamed broccoli with ume plum vinegar. These days, my mind clouded, my body craving deep salt. Mineral and green, or sweet and fat. Either-or.

Today, scrubbing surfaces makes me want to scrub inside.

Tonight, I cook dinner, sit down opposite my radio. A vase of fading yellow flowers to my left. I learn about the shape and operational strategy of the coronavirus while I sip my glass of cheap
~~~

French wine, my mason jar filled with filtered tap water. Listen as I chew my kale and frozen cauliflower sautéed with organic chicken sausage. This is my version of date night. It has been for a while.

I eat too little, drink too fast. Later, drunk, I trim my bangs over the sink.

~~~

The *New York Times* marks a milestone in the United States today: more than 100,000 cases of coronavirus. I read the news in bed, on my phone, then rise to look in the mirror.

Miraculous: the bang trim is even.

Gray and rain are soothing to me, folding in around this old apartment, blurry windowpanes. I begin to notice who my neighbors are, what they do for work. A grocery store cashier, a DoorDash delivery driver, a budtender. All of them young. Still going to work, still running up and down the stairs, still drinking indoors in the evening with their friends.

A former student lives above me with her boyfriend and their big gray cat. She works at the Safeway down the street. In college composition, as a freshman, she was quiet and a little sullen and wore black t-shirts and a choker necklace. She wrote an essay about art. Photography. That was five years ago. I wonder if she still takes pictures. I wonder if she will get sick. I think about the handles on the door to our four-plex, about the mail slots and the Safeway crowds. I think about her hands.

This rain. I want to hear the drip and still.

Antidote: a walk beneath some truly wild clouds and wind. Soaked, hair curled, my walk cut short. I hurry home to listen.

~~~

I emailed my primary care doctor to request an increase in my medication dosage. Since December, I've taken twenty-five milligrams of sertraline (generic Zoloft), generally considered to be half the standard clinical lowest dose. For a few months, it was enough to quell the unrelenting dizziness that had started interrupting my teaching, my driving, my ability to type. Lately, the haze is creeping in again. The tight breath. The blurred keyboard.

Last night I ate three pieces of whole-grain sprouted toast dunked in olive oil with salt, then sautéed a frozen Trader Joe's cauliflower rice bowl in the skillet and ate that, too.

In my dream, I was sick with Covid. I think I actually did wake up at one point with a microscopic scratch in the back of my throat, a bubble-headed feeling. Fear. Back asleep, the dream unspooled itself: I was sick, my dad was sick, my mom was rearranging mattresses, I was supposed to be going on a long drive and was drinking bourbon from a giant tumbler.

Today I'm down to my last pair of regular clean underwear. The rest, pink and cream and lace, all thongs. So pointless now.

Maybe I should get a cat.

~~~

April. A new month. Spring, and it is snowing out. I want to rearrange my bookshelves. Want to want to paint my nails.

Fennel salad.

Mopping, also, is a comfort.

~~~

Day two of the fifty-milligram dose. So far, mostly I feel calmer—though part of this I credit to the deeply cathartic experience of taking apart and deep-cleaning my vacuum yesterday, sweatpants covered with dust on the kitchen floor, nails dirt-black, hands filthy in a way that now feels newly safe. Using a screwdriver, dissecting parts, reassembling a body, and the satisfaction afterward.

Cleaning up.

This morning, I am reading articles from *The Cut* about dating in the time of pandemic social distancing. It's hard to imagine, or to get excited about, this sexting trend. As much as I've enjoyed it in the past with established partners, I can't fathom the performance energy it would require to date new people via Zoom and FaceTime, to think of something sexy and alluring to say to a stranger. Mostly I'm preoccupied with the very real possibility of losing my job.

As for the urge to optimize—it comes and goes. I miss the tension: of wanting to improve, of the stakes for appearances being higher, the need for performance demanding discipline of me, of my body. But if that pressure, that necessity goes away, what might appear in its place?

In bed, I scroll through the news and end up following links to ads for bamboo bidet attachments.

On the radio, they say the number of U.S. cases is now more than 290,000.

I text my mom. She says she feels numb, like crying. We postpone our phone date. I make matcha, gather trash.

~~~

The workday begins. Peeling away, day by day, the usual structures.

Standing in the kitchen. I'm listening to *The Daily* from September 18 and 19, 2020. Lisa Bloom and Gloria Allred. The ways in which Allred and the legal system and the need for power and attention silenced women on the wrong side of celebrity and time.

I'm thinking of my mother. Her dinner with Allred in 1978, at a Hamburger Hamlet somewhere in Hollywood, in the days before the hearing for her rape case. That she'd had to defend the fact that she was sexually active prior to the attack because, back then, such behavior outside of marriage—regardless of context—was considered cause for assault.

The way she shocked the judge by using the word "coitus" instead of "sex" to describe what had happened.
~~~

"You stumped him," Allred had told her afterward.

At dinner, they'd ordered salads and wine.

~~~

Scrolling through social media, a paid post—an ad for shoes, I recognize the brand—catches my eye:

Fashion is about agency and choice.

The ad calls this ethos "the new fashion statement," and the company (I know from Instagram ads, from friends) makes shoes from recycled plastic materials. They are simple flats, spectacularly expensive. I think about agency and choice and optimization. About fashion, beauty, and feminism. Privilege leveraging the language of freedom versus oppression.

And now, all of it stripped away.

This morning, Bernie Sanders ended his 2020 presidential campaign.

~~~

What does power even mean?

Ordered a fancy takeout burger with provolone and a side kale Caesar salad. Inhaled it at my kitchen table, ravenous. Also today: watered plants, chopped onions, did laundry, vacuumed, cleaned the windowsills. My period is five days late, but since I haven't had sex since December, I'm pretty sure it's the pandemic's fault.

~~~

Finally started bleeding, just a smudge this morning after breakfast. Stayed in bed late, came twice, felt the pleasure then the pain wave through my lower abdomen, then ebb as I made coffee. Next, finished reading eighty-seven residency applications. I'm jurying for
~~~

the arts center where I wrote the first draft of my graduate thesis, which feels at once very professional and very bureaucratic.

Three squares of salty dark chocolate and cold brew coffee in a blue-flecked mug.

Now the sunshine. I unfold my knees, roll my shoulders. Time to go outside.

Baked chicken tenders with paprika and plated like I used to at the restaurant: large white bowl, piled rainbow chard and sautéed onions, chicken stacked on top. I sent photos to my parents, feeling proud. Neither texted back.

On *The Daily*, they are interviewing a woman who has been living out of her car. Washing her hair from a water jug. Waiting for a job interview at the grocery store.

I measure out the last 2.5 ounces of natural wine, French, from last week's impulsive online purchase. Decant into a big glass so I can swirl, sniff, and taste the width of it—the flavor, how it opened. The thing is, I cannot afford the wine. Family and good credit operate like friendly ghosts. I am deeply lucky—privileged. Dessert is toast. Cheaper wine, bigger pour. On the radio they say the state university where I teach wants our quarantine diaries for an archive. I feel private, protective about these pages. I suspect that is my ego as a writer getting in the way. Or else, just my ego.

~~~

Dreamt I made some kind of a pie filling in the blender. Pumpkin?

~~~

Feels important to get dressed today. Shower, wash my hair. Three Zoom meetings this afternoon, and the endless push-pull between inspiration and ennui, the struggle to motivate beyond my bed, my room, my apartment. I grind coffee, squeeze a quarter of a lemon into a cup, and think about fall classes while I listen to the news.

Through the window, I watch my neighbor walk slowly down to his basement garden office, a folder of documents and a coffee cup in hand, pink-collared shirt beneath a black sweater, bright white hair.

I've spent the past three nights staying up late, watching swashbucklers I loved as a teenager and their shitty sequels. *The Mummy, The Mask of Zorro*. I'd been so in love with Brendan Fraser and Antonio Banderas in the late 1990s.

Sleeping in until nearly 9 a.m. to catch up on rest.

Wired up on coffee, weighted down with peanut butter. Friday. Sunshine, high of sixty-two. I wish I felt like caring how I look today. Woke up feeling sorry for myself, then loathsome about feeling that inclination amid so much privilege.

Need to wash my hands. That peanut butter smell.

On my walk earlier, I was startled by the sight and sound of an airplane overhead.

Making supper. Every time I grill tilapia in the skillet, it smokes up my apartment. Now I am eating, hiding, in my office, all of the other windows flung wide and my tiny fan running in the dining room.

~~~

Yesterday I cleaned the house, scrubbed the bathroom walls, put winter socks and scarves in storage, organized my hall closets, dusted baseboards.

These past few days I've felt haunted by old loves. Softly haunted: pleasant memories.

~~~

Falling asleep last night, I found myself recalling the summer after starting college when Peter and I finally dated for a few short weeks. That day when it began, in San Francisco, wandering the Haight, and how he let me rest my head on his shoulder on the BART train as we headed home; that evening at his house, watching *In America* on his funny twin bed. I was wearing my Old Navy California t-shirt, white and thin. That would have been the summer of 2004. I was nineteen. I'd imagined myself in love with Peter, off and on, since my junior year of high school. Driving home that night, playing back the feeling of his arm around my shoulders, his lips on mine, his hands along the thin white cotton of my shirt—it must have been utterly unlike anything I had yet felt in my life.

I'd been kissed before, touched before, but never by someone I'd harbored secret feelings for the way I had with Peter. I wish I could remember better; but in a way, I'm also pleased to find the memories blurred out. It's sweeter that way. Fewer questions. Easier to fall asleep.

~~~

One month of distance instruction.

There is a heaviness inside me. I want to do something, change the sensation, but it's becoming clear that no quick fix will do. That this may be the state of things, back and forth, for several years. That "normal" isn't something I, or we, can count on getting back.

Smoked herbal cigarettes in my bathroom tonight. Now can't edge the smell. Afterward, danced so hard—alone, with headphones, in my living room—that I woke up with a blister on my toe. Bad sleep. Kept imagining the click of the fan to be rain against my window.

~~~

I turned off the alarm, went back to sleep, and dreamt that the dean of our college was unloading wine shipments and popping champagne bottles on campus, that he invited me to taste but I was trying to prepare for a presentation that involved some writing I had done inspired by an old VHS tape of my mother's that I'd also edited to superimpose text on the moving images. My old poetry professor was there, and that made me nervous. I was underprepared. I said, "No, thank you," to the wine.

My underwear is hanging up to dry across the shower-curtain rod. All windows are open, and the birds are out.

~~~

Second-to-last day of distance instruction. More than 1 million cases of Covid-19 in the country. It is difficult to feel motivated. I want to tell my students to just rest.

Feel fantastic this morning, despite disrupted sleep—a hot sweat in the middle of the night, restless waking dreams, no recollection of the narratives. Drinking coffee with coconut oil, blended. My eyes burn but I feel vaguely invincible.

I think back to that night in the red apartment building on Polk Street. Not yet single, newly living alone. Five years ago. October. Drinking rye and soda, listening to Billie Holiday, hanging pictures on the wall and rearranging furniture. That thrill. A new cotton dress. The promise of voyeurs or dinner guests someday.

This oscillation: yesterday, malaise; today, motivation. Impossible to predict.

~~~

Anxiety management in the form of 24,000 steps yesterday, to the point of dizzy hunger. What am I steeling myself against? Sameness, of course, for one thing (hence the rearranging of furniture, online shopping), but also the need to sustain myself and reinvent in solitude and quiet. No stage.

I am worried about my mom.

~~~
~~~

Last night I watched *Two Days in Paris* and hated it. What was it I saw there when I went to the arthouse cinema in Berkeley by myself and watched it then, in 2007, when it first came out? Was it simply the French? The atmosphere? Or was I just *that* young?

I think about my sense of fear around sex, and also my sense of power. Because I cannot help it, though I wish I could, this also makes me think about my mother. How sex and love together feels most dangerous—and of course, I have been given this: a history of violence, of fear, of betrayal, of romantic disappointment, from my mother. Again, by myself: my own actions, relationships.

Where does control reside? What is the price paid for agency? How are the two similar and different?

I look up all the words online. Power predicates agency. Control requires influence over another, or the self, but suggests limitations, restrictions. Freedom is the opposite: to move or speak without hindrance.

~~~

I think about how my mom always says things like "that's a meal!" about anything that fills her up—two bites of an avocado, a piece of buttered toast—in a way that makes me feel ashamed for eating more than she does, even though I'm taller and move so much more frequently and faster every day. How she has, for decades, saved her calories for wine. How I have lately done the same.

Her inadvertent complicity with body shaming; the way both she and my father assess my figure.

My mother's mother was so small. So proud of her waist.

I walked all the way out of Moscow and back again this afternoon in the rain.

~~~

The Minneapolis police murdered a black man named George Floyd. The reports, the footage, are everywhere. Suddenly, it's summer:

hot and sunny. I feel a kind of limbo. Want to help and Idaho feels very red, very isolated. I find a list of actions in support of Black Lives Matter on the *Harper's* website. Also, a collaborative essay published in *Guernica* called "How We Drink Now."

Gray and hot and still today, with the odd breeze. I woke flushed and with a hint of sunburn on my left upper arm, the side most heavily in the sun on yesterday's trail walk.

Signed two petitions and donated to two separate funds in support of Floyd and Minneapolis protesters. Feels like less than a fraction of a drop in the proverbial bucket.

Tonight, met D in the park for a beer. I haven't seen him since Kristin's wedding back in December—that night, and the morning after.

At the time, I'd worried over complications. Said it was a one-time thing, and he'd agreed. *Just friends*. But now, sitting across from him at the picnic table, his smile is so warm, and his grown-out hair—curling a little, filling with gray—is very handsome. I realize I'm self-conscious. I keep touching my own hair, clean and down and flyaway, as we talk.

We left the park as the thunderstorm rolled in, millions of tiny dead leaves and petals blowing like a swarm of locusts or a sudden blizzard through the air and swirling in the street. Several got stuck in my hair.

As we parted ways, he told me that he liked my dress.

The spinning leaves. The thunder. That smile.

Back home, I felt so cinematic, standing at my window with my wine. I should learn to be wary of this feeling.

~~~

The nation is on fire. The virus continues to ebb and spread in odd patterns, and uprisings throughout America's cities threaten to spark a second wave sooner than predicted.

Last night I thought I slept well but my heart rate was up all night long.
~~~

No one I have been with has ever said I wouldn't let them in. What they have said is that I ask for too much.

~~~

Today, I woke up feeling woozy and unbalanced. Broken glass in the sink; half an herbal cigarette in a drawer.

I want very much to delete my social media accounts.

I wonder if I'd want kids if my mother was no longer alive.

I wonder where I'll put a litter box, a kitty bowl for water.

Approaching 2 million cases. Can't seem to quit with the unsettled sleep and difficult dreams.

~~~

Cases crossed the 2 million mark today and continue to worsen even as the country and world reopen.

Last night D touched my arm while we were sitting in the park again and I couldn't stop thinking about it but didn't know exactly why or what I wanted to come of all that thinking, feeling. I considered texting him. Instead, I drank too much gin and slept horribly and long.

~~~

Friday night. Mom called, in excruciating pain. She thought she might have another obstruction. She asked me to call 911. She couldn't talk long enough, clearly enough, to do it herself.

I made the call, met her at the hospital. We spent the next five hours in the ER with her obstruction (or something) acting up again. Whirlwind few days. Now she's home and resting, seems to be okay; I slept for hours and still feel sort of drugged. This is how it goes.

Best parallel parking job of my life at 2:45 a.m. on Saturday morning, home from the hospital. Amazing.
~~~

~~~

Mom is stable. Back to eating small amounts of solid food. Last night, to celebrate, I started my first foray into breadmaking.

Kneading sourdough this morning: open windows, singing birds, a soft gray light. Flutter of rain, dripping and landing against the eaves of the house. Hot coffee.

I think I understand about the bread. Why everyone is baking. The kneading, the texture, the rhythm, was peaceful. My hands were tired by the end of it.
~~~

A KIND OF CHRYSALIS

It is the first hot Friday afternoon in late May. I'm sitting on my mother's patio, eating carrot sticks and drinking a cold beer out of a can. Mom has watered-down box wine in a pint glass, filled up with ice. Together—six feet apart—we sit beneath a makeshift awning in our folding beach chairs. My pale legs sport an awkwardly visible ankle tan from two months' worth of walking and jogging outdoors in ⅞-length leggings. Mom is wearing a Dr. Seuss t-shirt and, as of this afternoon, is obsessed with detailing the size of the ants on her deck and the squirrels she talks to each and every day. She leaves them peanuts on the lawn and has taken to texting me photographs of one in particular, a scruffy-tailed, brazen little guy that just this morning nearly ventured into the apartment.

"He was staring me straight in the eye," she exclaims.

This is the same week George Floyd was murdered by a white policeman. Earlier this morning, Minneapolis burned in protest. Earlier last week, our Idaho town reopened restaurants, barber shops, and tattoo parlors, and at the grocery store nearly 80 percent of the patrons were clustering, unmasked. As of today, the nationwide caseload of Covid-19 surpassed 1.7 million. As of today, Trump is threatening to deploy the military to stem “the chaos.”

“I feel like I’m reliving the seventies in so many ways,” my mom writes via text earlier this morning. “An evil creep in the White House, intense foreign conflicts, economic craziness and terrible racial injustice and riots. I could see the smoke from Watts while it was burning.”

I wake up to her text message (this, the one prior to the photo of the squirrel). I wake up late. Another night of dark and heavy dreams. Such dreams are commonplace these days, apparently. *National Geographic* even published a study. My mother has been having dreams about being Chinese. I have been having dreams peppered with cameo appearances from every ex-lover imaginable. We are each intermittently glued to the news and avoidant of it. For the first month or so of the pandemic, I carried my little Bluetooth radio around the house with me, listened to *The Daily* with religious consistency on my walks around the neighborhood or while washing dishes after dinner. Lately, though, I’ve reached a saturation point. Perhaps it has something to do with the weather warming up, the desire to open all the windows every morning and listen to the breeze, the birds, instead of voices.

At night, I’ve taken to rewatching Jane Austen film adaptations from my youth. On my walks, I’ve been listening to their soundtracks, striking out onto the remote bike path that stretches out of town and into the neon green and yellow fields, the mountainous spun clouds of the Palouse. At thirty-five—single, in partial quarantine in a small semirural town where my daily walks and the very occasional distanced visit with my mother or with Sarah serve as the entirety of my social life beyond work-mandated Zoom meetings, living alone and suddenly taking an interest in domestic pursuits like baking, drawing, rearranging my bookshelves by color—I find my life closer to that of a housebound, middle-class Austenian heroine than ever before. Closer, that is, except for my age.

~~~

In her early twenties, my mother dropped out of community college for nearly eight months and stayed home recuperating from a drastic case of vitamin deficiency—a dietary imbalance that, left unchecked, had spurred deep depression, horrific skin lesions, and considerable malnutrition. During her convalescence, Mom watched the early PBS series *Elizabeth R*, starring Glenda Jackson, which first aired in the spring of 1971. I remember her telling me about the scenes that showed Queen Elizabeth scarred from smallpox, the impetus for her heavy white face makeup; about feeling a definitive kinship with both Elizabeth and Jackson as she sat at home on her parents' couch, tending slowly to her blistered skin. After that, she became, in her words, "addicted" to all things *Masterpiece Theatre*, PBS, and BBC.

The ensuing years would also find her at Otis, then at Cal State Northridge pursuing a master's in psychology (unfinished) before moving north to San Francisco from Los Angeles, marrying my father, and giving birth to me. Squarely in the middle of that timeline, there was the rape. She would pursue various spiritual paths to meaning and solace in those years, reading the I Ching and the Tibetan Book of the Dead. After my birth, she would finally, after much reluctance and previous disinterest, dabble in Christianity. She would read C. S. Lewis and find herself swayed. In doing so, she would also rekindle her love for any and all works by English writers.

When I was a toddler, Mom enrolled in literature classes at the local community college in Solano County, about halfway between our bayfront refinery town and the golden hills and ripe green vineyards of Napa Valley. Once a week, she attended evening seminars while I stayed at home with my father. He would hurry home from work, often running ten, fifteen minutes late, and then my mom would drive "like a maniac" to make it to her class on time. Despite a preference for movies over books when she was growing up, my mom came to love the classics that she studied
~~~

in those seminars. Most notable among them was Jane Austen's *Pride and Prejudice*.

This would have been in the late 1980s, long before Colin Firth or Helen Fielding or even Alicia Silverstone came along to propel Austen into the realms of the mainstream rom-com Hollywood machine. In fact, prior to this class, my mom had never read Austen, knew nothing of her novels, and had assumed the title referred to some kind of political treatise. While there are indeed critical elements of the political in all of Austen's novels, my mom was thrilled to find hilarious, acute, and realistic characters and social commentary at the core of her self-inflicted required reading.

My own introduction to Austen thus came when our familial evening television habits expanded beyond *Star Trek* reruns and *Faerie Tale Theatre* VHS tapes to include the 1980 version of *Pride and Prejudice*—a film so unwaveringly faithful to the literal text of the novel that much of the humor and pleasure of Austen's prose gets lost in the telling. I know this because I read the book not long afterward, probably around the age of nine. The 1995 BBC adaptation of *Pride and Prejudice*, starring Colin Firth and Jennifer Ehle and adapted for the screen by Andrew Davies, aired when I was ten. Young though I was, I came to the premier episode—together with my mother—with all the mingled thrill and skepticism of the most devout and seasoned Austenite.

~~~

For many years, I struggled to keep track of which was which: *entomology* versus *etymology*. The former is the study of insects; the latter, the study of words and their accumulated meanings, stemming from the Greek *eturnos*, meaning "true." Now, as an assistant professor of English myself, I finally have them straight. But this knowing is a recent definitive. And while I was usually seeking out the word related to language when I got the two confused, there remained something in the prosody, the texture of
~~~

the syllables—E-TY-MO-LO-GY—that, for ages, simply wouldn't sit right on my tongue.

As a child, I was afraid of bugs. Not spiders or anything specific so much as the general specter of the insect kingdom: their collective, insidious, lurking smallness. It would take me many years to sympathize. To scoop up errant visitors inside my car or apartment using Tupperware lids or paper scraps and try to set them free. To protect the moths that slip inside in search of light from the slow torture of my cat's paws. But even now, I still find myself defensive at times in the face of an unexpected house spider lurking in the sink. The fear returns. Fear: always looping back, like memory.

Words, meanwhile, were an early love. But it wasn't until I went to college and found myself mere steps away from the campus library—and, with it, the complete and unabridged *Oxford English Dictionary*—that I truly began to appreciate their power.

~~~

I got my mom a Roku for Christmas last year. A and I had owned one, so I was familiar with the setup. I remember hoping that my experience with Roku would prove that I was equal to the task of explaining the brand-new remote and channel-purchasing details to my mother, a determined technophobe. While I'd considered the gift for some time, I was worried that she would never use it. On the one hand, she was distinctly frightened of new gadgets. On the other, she frequently complained about how much she paid for cable and how few programs she actually wanted to watch.

Frustration in the face of her complaints won out. I spent the early part of Christmas Eve 2019 hunting down all her errant and outdated wi-fi passwords, fumbling with wires, and climbing underneath her dresser to take photos of the router data so I could set everything up. Once I finally succeeded, we celebrated with white wine and by arranging rosemary sprigs around a pork tenderloin roast. Afterward, we plopped the pork into the oven and settled in
~~~

for what was, quite possibly, our dozenth shared screening of the 1995 version of *Pride and Prejudice*. Several glasses of wine later, we had reached the critical dance scene between Elizabeth and Darcy, the scene I have come to think of as "the throwdown." Together, we paused the episode, put down our glasses, and stood facing one another in the living room. Given that I am roughly six inches taller than she is, I happily agreed to mirror Firth. We bowed, then giggled, then did our stumbling best to parallel the deceptively simple steps, laughing and bumping into one another until the oven timer chimed to let us know the pork was ready.

Eight months prior, I had been over to this same apartment for Easter. I'd walked to my mother's house that Sunday afternoon, stopping at the local organic co-op for a cluster of daffodils, a bottle of wine, and a yellow-frosted cupcake with delicate green sprinkles on the top. Hostess gifts, I suppose, or peace offerings. It was the first warm day in many months, warm enough for short sleeves without a sweater. I had considered wearing something long-sleeved and loose-fitting to conceal the new tattoo on my right triceps, but the sun was warm and the sky cloudless and anyway it seemed ridiculous to have to hide such a thing—this, my third tattoo, after all—from my mother, to try to keep it a secret as if I were a teenager who'd snuck off to get a stick and poke at summer camp.

As it turns out, my initial instinct had not been misplaced. If my mother had disliked my first tattoo and ignored my (admittedly small and subtle) second, expressing clear but passive disapproval and then mostly seeming to pretend they didn't exist, she positively reviled my third. I can still remember, with disturbing clarity, the look of horror on her face when I showed her the iteration of Louise Bourgeois's *Spiral Woman* stretching the length of my upper right arm. She turned her face away as if I had revealed a disfiguring mutilation.

Then she exploded. My mother called the image hideous, likening my spiral lady to a gigantic insect. She demanded to know why I had "ruined" my "pure, beautiful skin," then insisted that tattoos were classless, that they made me look "like trash." Over and over, she asked why I would do this to her and repeated that it was an act of disrespect, a sinful act, something designed specifically to hurt her and make her feel unwanted and unloved. I recall trying to sit through the bulk of this, taking deep breaths and shallow sips of wine, holding back speech. I didn't want to engage. To protest, I felt, would only appear to validate my mother's arguments. Subconsciously, I also did not want to admit that there *was* a modicum of truth, if not to my mother's anachronistic ideas concerning body art and class affiliation, then to my need to assert some independence and bodily control away from her sphere of influence. To make an irrevocable commitment to my own judgment and aesthetics beyond any associations with morality or virtue.

I did, at one point, try to explain the sense of control it gave me to choose and to wear something meaningful to me on my skin—something that perhaps did impact the presumed "purity" of my body (already a nonissue, since I had three other tattoos and my ears pierced, but whatever), an image that might not be conventionally "pretty," but that also made me feel like my own person, an agent beyond the pressure I so often experienced, especially as an adult woman, to follow the rules, to perform perfection. At this, my mother sneered.

"You're not *that* beautiful," she said. "Maybe you need to get over yourself."

~~~

Earlier this year, PBS's *Masterpiece* released the newest Austen adaptation: an eight-part episodic miniseries inspired by the author's final, unfinished novel. *Sanditon* aired in the United States in January 2020, mere weeks before the Covid-19 pandemic shifted from being frightening yet distant news out of China to taking over the lives and livelihoods of nearly everyone across the globe. My mother,
~~~

who regularly goes to bed at five or six in the evening, stayed up until nine to watch the premier.

Austen only finished eleven chapters of the novel, leaving a manuscript in which the story itself has scarcely begun. Multiple characters are introduced with only the slightest backgrounds, features, and context. The screenwriter only had so much to go upon. Then again, because that screenwriter was once again Andrew Davies (who, in the twenty-five years following his *Pride and Prejudice*, has become something of an Austen adaptation aficionado), skeptics and fans could at least trust him to know the author's tropes. While the show stays true to these—so much so, in fact, as to feel redundant and/or predictable at many a plot twist—the adaptation also drew mingled criticism and admiration from the press in response to Davies's integration of several contemporary and frankly sexualized themes into the fabric of *Sanditon*'s expanded narrative.

"Poor Jane must be turning in her grave!" my mother texted me the morning after the first episode aired on local public television.

Having read the *New York Times* review of the show, which mentions the presence of both skinny dipping and semi-incestuous innuendo in the show's early episodes and having likewise grown up with my mother's aversion to sex on screen in any context that isn't overtly humorous in a slapstick, *Monty Python* kind of way, I was not surprised at her reaction. At the same time, it was all I could do not to text her back: "Oh? And how do you know?"

Jane, with her acute observing eye and social savvy. Jane, with her profound understanding of the machinations of society and the pitfalls of the ego, vanity, and marriages either devoid of passion or built on nothing but. Jane, with her penchant for elopement between a very young woman and a very unworthy man as a plot device. Of course, she recognized the role of sex. Of course, she would have understood the incorporation of clear sexuality and sexual content in a twenty-first-century adaptation of her writing. At least, that is my take. I've read every novel, seen every cinematic adaptation, explored the JSTOR archives, written a handful of academic papers investigating Austen's subversive winks and gestures—in fact, often modeled my own after her example. Then again, what does any of that matter? It's not like I was there. I'm not an Austen scholar, and neither is my mother. I know my mother's aversion has little to do with assumptions of Jane Austen's naïveté.

Sex and sexual machinations exist and always have. More often than we'd like, they're related to money, to power, to control. Three subjects Jane knew intimately. No matter how well hidden, the sex was always present in her marriage-centric novels.

Last week, I finally ran out of familiar Austenian fare to rewatch on my laptop and opted for a PBS *Masterpiece* subscription so I could see *Sanditon* for myself. What followed was, admittedly, a bit of a binge-watching obsession, fueled as much by Rachel Barrett's lively and supremely walkable soundtrack (and—yes, I confess—a waistcoat-clad, horseback riding Theo James) as the narrative itself. The plot revolves around Charlotte Heywood, the well-read daughter of a provincial farmer, who happens upon an invitation to spend the season in the titular seaside town of Sanditon with Mr. Tom Parker and his wife. Parker, a sort of mastermind of the town project—an entrepreneur who is building apartments and planning events, determined to lure London's fashionable sea-bathing vacationers—has a silly brother, a silly sister, a handsome and mysterious brother, and a saint of a wife. He also has a wealthy patroness among the local landed gentry, and his brother has a ward in the figure of Miss Lambe, a half-black heiress from the West Indies with a fortune to her name, likewise newly arrived in town.

For three nights in a row, I camped out on my living-room floor with my computer on my lap and a slice of toast and large glass of wine close at hand, utterly engrossed, forgetting the time, staying up past midnight. While the end of season 1 is clearly designed to leave viewers wanting more, I was surprised at the depth of my frustration, an unsettled feeling bordering on depression, in response to the conclusion of the show. On the night I finished watching, I slept fitfully. On the next night, I started the series over again, determined to unpack this strange, persistent triggering effect *Sanditon* was having on my psyche.

~~~

My undergraduate major, declared almost immediately, was English and American literature. This meant I had ample opportunity to perfect my practice of turning to the *OED* for nearly every single essay assignment. From Milton and Shakespeare to eighteenth- and nineteenth-century novels, from the Modernists and Beats to Didion and DeLillo, I read carefully, plucking words from their verses and sentences, holding them up to the light. I dug, inspected, probed, and cataloged. I was looking for secrets and often found them in the most archaic and enigmatic of my subjects—Milton, Fielding, Dickinson, Pope. And despite an eventual shift in scholarly allegiance toward more contemporary fare, nearly all my early forays into critical writing found their stride amid the older stuff, the novels I'd grown up reading and watching in the form of *Masterpiece Theatre* and BBC adaptations.

These older texts held the strangest words, the weirdest histories; and, often, the best ground for taking control of an argument. The more modern the slang, the more meaning one could imagine or erase from the author's intent. But once upon a time, the secret codes and subversive hints had been definitive, precisely because they had been newly written. Newly understood, and only by a certain few. Uncovering such clarity gave me a singular sense of control on the page. In the company of peers who found etymology boring or archaic, I felt as though I'd discovered the perfect weapon: actual truth, boiled down.

Looking back at my undergraduate self, so full of vulnerabilities, so unwilling to risk an opinion without factual ballast in even the most casual of conversations, I suspect that I was desperate for some grounding: a sense of objectivity in a rapidly expanding field of experiences and confusions. To carry the multiple meanings
~~~

of a word in my pocket—quite literally, back then, as I'd heave open the print *OED* in the reference library, settle in, take notes by hand—and spool them out in a strategic order as I spun each new literary analysis essay, gave me a sense of agency, lent my writing an orderliness within the efforts I never failed to make in support of subtly subversive, feminist readings of classical texts. Putting Milton's serpent in conversation with Dickinson; reading *Gatsby* through the cynical, proto-feminist character of Jordan Baker.

I had always been a rule follower as a child. I got straight As, went to Sunday school, did my homework, won awards for citizenship and scholastic promise. As I got older, I kept this up: no smoking, no drinking, no parties, no piercings, no sex. I went to dances with permission and a ride to and from with my parents. I spent my allowance on alternative rock CDs and cheap t-shirts from Target. With a few notable exceptions, I continued my collegiate career in this same vein. I wasn't consciously trying to be good, I don't think, at least not in any religious sense, but I was certainly subconsciously trying to please my parents; to make sure I never failed at earning the pride, affection, and financial support they seemed to delight in providing me with as I kept up appearances, kept achieving. This, I must have felt, was the unspoken agreement.

When I finally did begin to test the boundaries of my experience, to explore little rebellions, I had a tendency—perhaps in part due to the influence of my lawyer father and the high school summers I'd spent working in his office, or perhaps it was the inefficacy of ugly yelling and door slamming my mother often demonstrated when it came to their domestic arguments—to enact them quietly, deftly. To take the instructions, written or implied, and follow them so well as to find their loose points and then exploit them in favor of my argument. Only now, halfway through my third decade, can I finally begin to see not only the false subversion of this approach, the very clear adherence to existing power structures inherent in all of my minor revolts, but also the undertones of vengeance.

On my part, a resentful temper. I wanted recompense for all that unsung time spent being good.

~~~

The word *pupa* comes from the Latin *pūpa*, meaning "doll." I won't deny that the rounded, looping torso of the *Spiral Woman* recalls the shape of an insect in the pupal stage or that her simplistic, cartoonish arms, legs, and head are distinctly doll-like—more ragdoll, though, than Barbie doll. And this is what I love about her: that she is at once stunning and grotesque, a floating child-woman strung up tight yet with hair that floats and billows, defying gravity. When my tattoo artist, Karla, underestimated the time our session would take, it was because of the hair. So much of it, such intricate linework. The design took nearly four hours to complete to Karla's satisfaction.

The woman's sculpted, undulating hair. Her dangling legs. Visually, and perhaps associatively, these are my favorite aspects of the *Spiral Woman's* black-ink body. To me, they represent the freedom half of the spiral equation put forth by Bourgeois: "The spiral—I love the spiral—represents control and freedom." But I am also an imperfect body, aging and bumpy and bruised and flushed and lined in places I wasn't only several years ago. I am thirty-five years old and showing it. I am no longer some young romantic heroine fresh to the world, a story waiting to happen. For this, then, I also love the *Spiral Woman*'s contradictions and her ugliness. Her imperfection, as a woman in a body. Her vulnerability and her power twisted together.

"Spirals," Bourgeois writes, "—which way to turn—represent the fragility in an open space. Fear makes the world go round."

~~~

Mom goes inside, brings us back a string cheese each. Something prepackaged and safe for sharing. I "wash" my hands with the sanitizer I keep in my purse, then peel the wrapper open two-thirds of the way and eat the cheese stick in three solid bites. No strings.

We are debating the merits and pitfalls of the *Sanditon* series. I agree that there is too little of the signature Austen humor in the characters for it to feel genuine, that it is too much soap opera, not enough sitcom. But I disagree with her stance on the emphasis, in Davies's adaptation, on elements of race, gender, and sex—and how all three are tied inextricably to money. As noted in the *New York Times* review of his 1995 *Pride and Prejudice*, superficial preoccupation with things like lace and ribbons, carriages and hat making, belies not only the satirical wit but also the frank and clear-eyed awareness with which Austen revealed the economic cogs driving the social matchmaking machine—an awareness, it seems, that alarmed sophisticated readers like the poet W. H. Auden when they realized, in reading her novels, just how sharply Austen understood her gendered predicament.

The horror. That a man should find himself disturbed by a woman's accurate, unvarnished acknowledgment of money and power as drivers of inequity, racism, and sexism.

Of course, Auden's discomfort, like the importance of money in many an Austenian marriage plot, is tied to fear. For Auden, perhaps, fear that more and more women might likewise see their circumstances plainly and revolt. For Austen's heroines, fear of spinsterhood (not so bad in theory, very terrible if it meant being stuck with your parents forever unless you happened to like your parents and have a decent allowance, a modicum of freedom), of failing to support their families, of damaged reputations that would ripple and loop out and around each member of a tainted family.

I want to say that it's different now, that things *have* changed, that our collective eyes are opened. But for most of us—societies, families—reputation and money and class and the restraint of women and the manipulation of their bodies, via sex or fashion or violence, still matter very much indeed. It's not hard to decipher the subtext of the Regency fashions that pervade the set of *Sanditon*;

the series star Rose Williams herself alludes to their significance in an interview for *The Times of London*: flowing gowns and artfully styled hair on the surface, tight corsets underneath.

"Consider just how many instances of conniving, possibly too-close brother and sister pairs there are in her books," I say, taking a swig of my beer. Mom spots another giant ant on the deck and squashes it with a piece of scrap paper pulled from the trash. I proceed to list my evidence. "The Crawfords in *Mansfield Park*, the Thorpes in *Northanger Abbey* . . . all kind of *too* cozy, you know? The Denhams"—here referring to the sexual tension between a stepbrother and sister in *Sanditon* as they conspire for their aunt's fortune—"are just part of that same pattern, played up a bit. And it is always about marriages or money or inheritance."

Mom rolls her eyes but doesn't argue. Instead, she shifts topics. "And what about the black girl? Did Jane actually write about her?"

I bristle. Miss Lambe was, famously, Austen's first and only primary black character. I'm certain that my mother knows this, or at least that once upon a time she did.

"Yes, she did." I know my voice is sharp, but I continue. "They say it was poised to be her most modern novel, focused totally on self-made men and centralizing the story of an heiress whose mother was a slave." I can hear the pedantry dripping from my mouth but can't make myself stop. It is one of my biggest grievances: when my mom plays dumb about these things, things she herself taught me to care about. A grief more than a grievance with the passage of time and the dawning realization of a change—in my mother's memory, in her ability to engage beyond herself. In many ways, she is still so sharp. But some things are starting to diminish. Sometimes, when I think that I am angry or annoyed, I realize later that I'm frightened.

"I've always found it strange that Austen never really talked about the Napoleonic wars . . ." Mom trails off, turns to watch an enormous crow pluck a peanut from the sidewalk, then fly to the neighbors' roof to peck at the shell. The conversation about race, about Miss Lambe, is over before it has begun. I'm getting even more irritated now. As much of a stretch as it may seem, I'm recalling the mantra I have read over and over in the news today: *His name was George Floyd. Say his name.* Again, I know my mother has heard it, too.

"She includes soldiers and sailors in nearly every novel," I counter. "Just because she isn't commenting on the war overtly doesn't mean it isn't on her mind. Maybe slavery was more front and center, more of a priority. It shows up in *Mansfield Park*, too."

"Yes, I remember that from the movie," she replies, shaking her head. "It was disturbing. I didn't like that version. I don't go to Jane Austen to be disturbed. I want something fun, something witty."

I know the scene my mother is alluding to, a scene in the 1999 *Mansfield Park* theatrical release that suggests, via a series of sketches that poor relation Fanny Price stumbles upon while caring for her sick cousin, that his father, her otherwise kindly benefactor Sir Thomas Bertram, not only owns and beats slaves on his Antigua sugar plantation but condones—perhaps even participates in—the rape of female slaves as well. It is, indeed, disturbing. So is slavery. I say as much, more quickly and sharply than I had intended.

Later that evening, back in my own apartment, I consider. My mother's resistance to overt reality—racism, sexual predation—in her sanctified Jane Austen canon, a world of PG romance and surface elegance she insists is not only more authentic but also "classier" than contemporary adaptations, upsets me. Then again, this time we've spent together during the pandemic, the forced time apart during the colder months, when being together felt too dangerous, has heightened my awareness of my mom's increasing social isolation, her advancing age, her sensitivities. When she resists disturbing content in the media, I wonder if her tolerance, particularly in the face of the Trump administration's daily atrocities, has simply given out. If her own traumas—from the rape in the 1970s to the seemingly constant onslaught of surgeons' hands, the IVs, invasive inspections, and difficult medications with which doctors have pummeled her body in the months and years leading to 2020—have effectively obliterated any part of herself that can stand to bear witness.

Everyone in the world is desperately seeking solace in the face of the pandemic. For my mother, that solace takes the shape of midmorning sherry and Jacques Pepin cooking shows, shopping online for vintage blouses she'll never wear and staying up late with YouTube Bible study videos playing on her iPhone. There is a safety in remaining on the surface of things: pretty, arty, flowy, sweet. Perhaps, at this point in her life, it is all she can take.

~~~

Corsets bear a complex history. Whether they were considered primarily supportive or destructive depends on the source. A cursory exploration of the corset reveals everything from allegations of internal organ damage and respiratory disease to avowals of structural benefit and back support while completing domestic chores. And, of course, there's the underlying issue of female restraint. The body, pinched in. Tightened and controlled.

Regency fashion has always intrigued me. The dresses like Ionic columns, simple and straight with minimal adornment at the torso. Compared to the Corinthian splendor of each era sandwiching the one in which Jane Austen's heroines lived and dressed, these gowns seem—as I am sure they were intended to—akin to Roman togas. Classical, refined. I always thought such gowns appeared so elegant and easy in the movie versions of Austen's novels: straight skirts and white cotton, uncinched and excellent for walking. But the giveaway is the bust. In an age prior to the push-up bra, the corset was there to do the work of elevation. Circling the unseen waist beneath that crisp white, restriction for nothing save the presentation of abundance at the breast. That Ionic shape: so narrow, so straight as to nearly be androgynous, but always with that telltale scroll at the top.
~~~

So often in Austen's novels, the markers of high fashion—satin, lace, an inside knowledge of the latest trend in long sleeves—demarcate social and economic standing. Similarly, the exposure of a character with money but no so-called breeding usually comes with a physical or fashion-centric faux-pas. Austen, to paraphrase her own Elizabeth Bennet, must "see as she finds." These markers are sometimes played for sarcasm, at other times for seriousness—whether to expose classist prejudices or superficial assumptions or, in both instances, the simple working of a social world swirling in silks and petticoats with the economy at its core.

For as long as I can remember, my mother has appreciated what she defines as "classy" women's clothing: usually vintage, from the 1930s through the 1950s, often menswear-inspired but tailored for a woman's body, frequently in the form of jackets, blouses, and two-piece suits. I remember her taking me shopping for something to wear to a middle-school class excursion to the San Francisco Opera. I was tall and suited to adult sizing, and my mother disapproved of nearly everything in the popular retailers—Hollister, Abercrombie & Fitch, Wet Seal—where my female peers shopped. She took me to Ann Taylor and bought a very minimally tailored, collard blouse. For shoes, practical Clarks with a low heel. High-quality fabric—a silk blend, I think—and leather, not at all inexpensive. But I loathed them, these clothes and shoes that seemed made to conceal anything feminine about my already tomboyish figure and awkwardly big feet.

If I've since grown into my own taste for tailored blazers and blouses, albeit with a preference for 1970s-era vintage and prints, I have also lived in the world of women and mothers and fashion and bodies and money long enough now to understand that class has nothing whatsoever to do with clothes unless you care how much those clothes cost—and not only that, but how casual an expense that cost might be to the owner.

The *OED* contextualizes *classy* as stemming from a particular subdefinition of *class*, pertaining to "groups, ranks, or categories," the origin of which comes from roughly 578 BC in relation to "a group of Roman citizens who could meet a certain minimum wealth qualification."[7] Later definitions proffer a more concerning overlap: "Of high or superior class, esp. stylish and sophisticated," or "Of, relating to, or characterized by classism; discrimination on the grounds of social class."

Trashy, meanwhile, is an easy one: "Of people: worthless, disreputable."

~~~

My mother and I were confirmed together. She was forty; I was seven. We'd been attending the local Lutheran church since I was in kindergarten, and my mom had become very involved, volunteering, assisting with communion and candles and vacation Bible school. For my part, I enjoyed Sunday school and my friends and the summer camps just fine. Framed as another social engagement and opportunity for art projects, putting on plays, and eating exotic snacks like Goldfish crackers and Fruit Roll-Ups forbidden in my mother's home kitchen, church activities were, for me, simply another addition to my social life and snack rotation. My dad wasn't very interested in church but would come every now and again on Sundays and at holidays like Christmas and Easter.

For years, Mom and I each took classes with Pastor Bob Nicholas: me, in the form of catechism during middle school; my mother, in the form of adult evening Bible study. Pastor Bob was, I must admit, damned cool. He was book-smart and clever yet down to earth, and eager to talk about the difficult questions that surround organized religion. My mother loved his willingness to delve into the history of the Bible, to conceive of it as a narrative, as a work of language as much as a book of law. How he would teach Bible

7 "Class" (noun), *Oxford English Dictionary*, 2010, https://www.oed.com. Reproduced with permission of the licensor through PLSclear.
~~~

study more like a literature seminar than instructions for seemly behavior and forgiveness. For my part, I grew to appreciate this, too—especially when I started at that private school across the bay, a Catholic school counterpart to my Lutheran catechism, and began to relish my double-agent role in religious studies classes, where I was already well versed in Luther's theses, all ninety-five arguments for institutional rebellion.

Things changed in my early teens, when Pastor Bob left, and a new pastor arrived from the Midwest to realign our little community Lutheran parish with the values of fundamentalism and the Missouri Synod. I do not remember the pastor's name. But I will never forget the day my mom announced she had lost interest in his services: "I spent the entire sermon thinking about taco recipes," she'd said in the car, on the way home. "I think that's probably a bad sign."

After that, Mom meandered from one denomination to the next for several decades. Nearly twenty years later, upon following me to Idaho in the wake of her divorce from my father and my own relocation for graduate school, she finally decided—not entirely out of nowhere, but unexpectedly all the same—to "convert" to Catholicism. I use scare quotes here because despite her confirmation at the local parish of St. Mary's, she stopped attending mass within a year. Her truest allegiance these days is still to Skip Heidzig and his YouTube channel, with countless hours of Bible study on tap for when my mom wakes up at night and can't go back to sleep. She keeps her phone nearby and listens for hours, lying in bed with the curtains drawn tight.

"I love how he will spend nearly half an hour on the roots of a single word from the scripture," she tells me over the phone, talking about last night's videos. It is midmorning, and we have both just confessed to still being in our pajamas. I am washing dishes and catching up on the news. "And that he tries so hard to avoid being political."

By this, she means that he resists addressing allegiances to President Trump or conservative politics, despite his close friendship and affiliation with fundamentalist church leaders across the country—a country currently divided on matters of racial inequality, white supremacy, police violence, and nationalistic political maneuvering. I understand why my mother, who hates Trump with a seething vitriol and struggles to (as Austen might have said) "keep her countenance" at the very mention of him (for shorthand, she calls him "butthead"), would want her chosen Bible study guru to avoid mention of our current commander-in-chief. Understand, especially, when she explains how she turns to Skip at night for comfort, when nothing else will do. At the same time, I listen to the news about her former church, Calvary Chapel of Chino, California, and the lawsuit her former pastor filed against actions banning religious gathering in a megachurch during a pandemic. I listen to the news about Trump's photo-op with a Bible and the pellet guns and teargas unleashed upon peaceful protestors in Lafayette Square. I listen to my mother explain to me that she is very much aware of Heidzig's friendships and allegiances within the church and—by extension—within the political machine. "But he doesn't bring it up," she says again, "and I just really admire that about him."

I want to call out what reads, to me, as Heidzig's blatant hypocrisy and cowardice, but I don't. I know the fight won't end well. Besides, in both the pastor's choice to smooth over potential conflict at the expense of justice and my mother's appreciation of it, I am struck by my own legacy of silence, of seemingly virtuous and sometimes manipulative acquiescence to the status quo, with an alarming and shameful clarity.

~~~

The pupal stage bridges the immature and mature iterations of certain insects. For butterflies, the pupa is called a chrysalis; for mosquitoes, a tumbler. Pupae may be further housed within additional, layered, protective structures such as cocoons, nests, or shells. Before reaching the pupal stage, those insects that undergo
~~~

a complete four-stage metamorphosis exist as larvae—from the Latin, meaning "ghosts" or "masks." If you have ever seen a picture of an insect in the larval stage, you can imagine the impetus for such a name: this small, ugly, shimmering, ephemeral body. This white child. Her spiral-shaped body will shed itself and harden into gold, tightening and dissolving before at last sprouting wings. But no transformation, no emergence, without this restriction first. The beauty and the cage.

Early in the pandemic, I bought myself a copy of *Louise Bourgeois: Spiral*, published by Cheim and Reid. It is a slim, beautiful coffee-table book of Bourgeois's selected spiral works and personal notes, journal entries, and poems reflecting upon this recurring theme in her paintings, drawings, sculptures, and textiles. The inside cover features copies of her own handwriting, in French, looped in spiral after spiral across a muted and seemingly coffee-stained sheet of blue paper. The portrait of the artist opposite the title page shows Bourgeois in angled profile, a geometric-patterned scarf encircling her neck, a spiral painting in the background, and her gloved hand, holding a paintbrush, in the fore. She is half smiling; a wry sort of smile, with heavy-lidded eyes and prominent lines of laughter, of living, rippling along her jaw and around her temples.

A favorite untitled piece: ink on paper, 1968. The spirals take a sort of insect or alien anatomical likeness. A thickly shaded oblong circle with a concentric, spiraling eye rests atop another thick oval. Black tentacles loop in and out and around this floating torso. Arms, scarves, smoke. There is a mysticism about this image. How it drifts in power. How its hands reach out of frame.

Unlike many drawings in the book, *Untitled, 1968* features not the usual "L. B." signoff but a crisp, legible signature. I wonder why.

On another page, a poem, dated 1970:

The room turns
with its little objects around me like
planets around the central sun—

before I was conscious of the walls and
I was constantly leaning against
them and feeling their strength
I feel a centrifugal force.
[...]
    control of the space
    grip on
    be sure of it because you need it

the center of gravity to change from
the container toward the contained.
the butterfly that flutters around the
lamp and all of a sudden the lamp
goes off, what is happening to it.

The chrysalis is an outer covering and a transitional state, protection while the pupa dissolves its immature body into a soup, all of those little spirals of the body melted down within a golden shell in order to transform; grow wings. Move beyond.

~~~

Several days later, I will feel dizzy all afternoon. I will make a simple dinner—cooked greens, fried eggs, a glass of beer—and sit down near the radio. I will tune it first to the market news, in which the analytical focus of the day is the link between social unrest and economic precarity (with an emphasis on comparison with the Rodney King riots in Los Angeles), then to *The Daily*, which will cover the one-week-later retrospective on the riots in Minneapolis and beyond. I will hear the footage I have missed: I will hear more than enough with just my ears. I will lean against the kitchen counter and start to cry.

It will be on this same day, on a long walk along the bike trail, that I will realize what it is about *Sanditon* that has its claws in my
~~~

throat. It is that the story is not, in the end, like Austen at all. It is not a comedy of manners that ends in happy marriage. It is more realistic—and yes, therefore, less funny, more disturbing—than that. It is a story in which the economic system in place positions first black people, then women, and ultimately even men at the mercy of its arbiters. It is a story in which illness and uprising and slavery and sexual abuse and labor injustice and licking flames all conspire to keep lovers apart, keep women in the role of property, keep men in check lest they threaten the status quo and lose their privilege by refusing to adhere. It is a story in which the feckless entrepreneur who would succeed and expand at the cost of his workers' safety and security, the cost of his wife's trust and his children's future, the cost of his benefactor's health and his own brother's happiness, is the only character who ultimately wins.

Sanditon's heroine, Charlotte Heywood, is young. Played by Rose Williams, a beautiful actor with a tanned complexion, light freckles, a snub nose, loose curls, and an ample bust, she appears—especially cast opposite the tall, dark, angular, and considerably older Theo James—even younger. I'm sure I notice this, in part, because of my own age. I am the same age as James, in real life, when I first watch the show. But there is also the issue of my students, an oft-rotating cast of eighteen- to twenty-one-year-old women with whom I work and talk and whose essays, far too often involving the impact of anxiety, trauma, or sexual assault upon their bodies and minds, I read and read and read and read and read. Before the pandemic, one of my brightest and most excited Honors students suffered a concussion. She confided in me the reason: a sexual assault. Sitting together in an empty dining hall, dimly lit, she told me what had happened. She was, is, only one of many with a similar story.

Part of me sees Williams's Charlotte and envies her overt, plump-skinned youth. Part of me observes that youth and worries, wants to wrap her body up in scarves and buttoned collars, to protect her from these older men and all the ways their choices, when it comes to loving her or not, may have less to do with her personhood or with her body than with money, with power, with their own financial or psychological insecurities.

If Charlotte's story is too contemporary, it is also too timeless. In my worry for her body and her heart, I suspect I see the flicker of my mother's worry for my body and my soul.

Many months later, I will meet with a freshman student—another woman, another member of the Honors College, sharp and funny and sarcastic with long shinning hair and a tall angular body I recognize from my own youth. This woman will tell me that her passion for exploring her world and her relationship to spirituality, a quest she has recently embarked upon after leaving organized Catholicism for something self-made involving awe of nature, an intrinsic belief in the power of fungal networks and the microbiome, has stalled because she was out at night in the same area where a shooting took place on our state university campus. Because, she tells me, in those blank unspeakable moments after the lockdown alert and before any assurance of safety, the fear, the uncertainty, the trauma of that moment took it all away: her passion, her desire to explore.

"I just can't get interested in things the way I did before," she says, her scuffed sneakered feet crossed, her head down. "I faced the possibility of everything ending and I . . . now I just can't."

I know my mother, ever since she has been my mother and probably long before, has only wanted to protect me. Perhaps we can only actively protect that which we have learned—via observation, via violation—to fear losing; to value because it can so easily and senselessly be lost.

"Beginning at the outside is the fear of losing control," Bourgeois writes of the spiral. "The winding in is a tightening, a retreating, a compacting to the point of disappearance."

My mother fears for my body and my soul because she has had to fear for hers, far too many times. Perhaps there are stories I don't know about her life before me, stories where the question of class and worth, of financial assets and personal value, were more enmeshed than I realize. Or perhaps these stories are echoes of my mother's mother's life, a life of extreme poverty and loss that finally, after a so-called good marriage, turned stable. Perhaps the worst of it is when my mother and I have these talks and seem to resolve them in a reconciled, peaceful place, only to then see them resurrected several months later. Her memory, I worry, beginning to slip. Her anxiety taking over: "Yes, yes, but I don't *remember* and I need to talk to you about your immortal soul . . ."

I, in turn, fear for my heart. For my own—these days, a lonely heart—and for my mother's, too frequently broken. For body worry, I turn to those dear to me—my mother, my students, my little cat. Of course, I fear for my own body, too. But it is a different kind of worry. An operational concern: sleep levels, caffeine levels, vitamin levels, alcohol levels. I use my body to move through the day, and my brain to power much of my work. I likewise use my brain to neutralize or conceal my body's vulnerabilities whenever I need to in order to survive. I choose clothes or a walking pace or a method of eye contact or a sexual partner with the reactive mechanisms of a defensive driver. I am always on the lookout for my heart, that it not be broken. Bruised, fine. Touched, fine. But never broken.

It has taken years for me to see this. For me to see the layers, patterns, within which my mother and my grandmother and I have operated our bodies in the world, our minds and artistic inclinations on a page or canvas or hunk of clay.

Now, I suspect, we are at a crossroads. My grandmother, long passed away. My mother, nearing seventy. Myself, old enough to count the new gray hairs when they appear in the harsh overhead light above my bathroom sink. I can't argue with my mother about my soul. I think I believe that we probably all have one—or, in other words, I'm still working out exactly what I believe and therefore my thinking requires much qualification. I get frustrated when Mom lectures me from her Bible study or Catholic catechisms, want to remind her (and sometimes slip up, do) that I was raised with all of this: Bible, church, confirmation. That I spent my child and young adulthood with one foot skimming the surface of Lutheran doctrine and the other sunk deep into the complexity and lore of Catholic church history. Do I remember everything I studied then? No. Do I feel devoid of context for understanding the values and pitfalls of organized religious affiliation and faith? No. Does my mother despair for my eternal fate after many, many hours of YouTube Bible study? Yes. Can I fix it? No.

"Beginning at the center is affirmation," writes Bourgeois. "The move outward is a representation of giving, and giving up control; of trust, positive energy, of life itself."

Each day at a time. Increasingly, I think, this is all we have. Some forward motion. My reaching outward, even if she curls away.

INTERLUDE: BRUSHWORK

2022

The new landlords agreed to paint the walls, any color of my choosing. Ever since, I've been hesitant to touch them. Resisted making marks or holes. The apartment walls, once multicolored—charcoal gray, Pepto pink, mermaid blue—are now a warm and uniform off-white. Like the inside of a crème brulée after spoon cracks molten sugar, browned.

I have loved to crack the sugar. I used to torch brulée at work, to do it badly. Burning sugar with a balanced hand and even keel takes practice. It was a short-term job. Before they burned, early in my shift, I'd set the chilled brulée out on a sheet pan, cover them with plastic—gingerly, to keep their surfaces unmarred. Until it burns, the cream must lie quite still. Cold and still. Inviolate.

Getting older causes changes to the skin. It is summer. Heat and sun, sweat and oil. I keep buying makeup, each formula and color scarcely different despite the variance in price. Maybelline, Neutrogena, Bare Minerals, Nars. Classic Ivory, Nude, Golden Light, Alaska. It is as if my undertones have changed. My face, a heat map. The dark circles beneath my eyes, the little flushed specks along the apples of my cheeks, the cat-scratch skin along my wrist, the blooming five-finger bruise on my right triceps—each of them, it seems, require minor shifts in color, texture, to conceal.

One tattoo is an initiation. Two, then three, and suddenly the body is a canvas. It depends on where they land, where you place them, where the artist puts their hands. I didn't know that this would happen. But now that I have four, each piece is no longer a stand-alone idea. The images begin to speak to one another. The blank spots beg for ink.

A finger-pattern bruise appeared this morning, blooming. I didn't feel it when it happened, but the sight of those blue marks beneath my Spiral Woman *tattoo, beneath her floating body, frightened me. Like the man the night before had frightened me. Something tight like string that told me it was wise to be afraid. The man was very big and very strong, strong enough to lift and hold me up, my legs around his waist. Strong enough to scare me when he bent me over after, leaned his body into mine and whispered, "I could push inside you now, so easily."*

I pierced the wall to hang a painting, framed, above the fireplace. It is always difficult, I find, to make the first commitment, mark. Then it gets easier. This one is an ocean scene, a thrifted piece with heavy oil paint, strong strokes and knife work. Rough waves and jagged rocks. My first tattoo is likewise of the coast: a Monterey cypress, wind-beaten, reaching for the sea. The image like a watercolor in its elegance, its weight. Nothing like the heavy Spiral Woman, her floating body bloated, held to thick black arms and legs despite her rising, wild mane of hair. Both reside on my right arm, a biceps's stretch of unmarked skin between them.

This arm is turning into something: an inventory, an irreversible collage. A space to receive the ink and hold it there, beneath the surface of the skin. What happens next is as much a matter of placement as it is a matter of symbology, design.

Choosing where to puncture is everything. That first moment, or the moment just before: your hovering spoon, the perfect wreckage of burnt sugar. Letting your eye take in this landscape, scorched to caramel because you asked. Hovering. Deciding what it is you want to break.

PENTIMENTO

May 2021–*June* 2022

1.

Sun melts the curtains, melting and pooling first along the wood, then woven wool. The new apartment has west-facing windows, transforming each late afternoon into a symphony of yellow light. Your cat, Lou, alternatively slinks into these sun puddles and licks the soft fur along her belly or the inside of a leg, then moves to the cooler, shaded patches of the hardwood and spreads, her body long and unexpected in its reach. She's like a little piece of furniture. Yet another new and now intransient presence. She wriggles, stretches all her darling pink and perfect black, black toes. You watch her claws extend, then quiver, then contract.

2.

Lou was only one year old and weighed a scant five pounds when you adopted her last summer. At the Humane Society they told you she was essentially a teen mom, found feral with a litter of kittens. Suckling their tiny mouths had sucked her dry.

Your first night together, Lou hid beneath the couch for hours. You coaxed with random cat treats purchased blindly at the local Petco, drank two beers, too nervous to eat anything yourself. After dark, she emerged and crawled onto your lap. You sipped carefully then, afraid of disturbing her, of disturbing this: your precious newness, her body trusting yours.

All night long, she explored the apartment, running and hunting for shadows, knocking down books, squeezing and contorting her slight body under dressers, desks. You never truly slept until daybreak, staying up instead to listen with all the intensity and worry you imagined overcomes mothers with their newborns that first night home from hospital. Responsibility and love enormous overhead, like clouds.

At last, sometime near dawn, Lou clambered onto the pillows beside you and slept in an indescribable pose: head tilted upward, toes and feet splayed forward and occasionally overhead. When you woke, you stroked the tiny striped patch of fur between her ears as gently as you could.

3.

Because your mother went to art school in the seventies, you trust her judgment when she says it's one of your best paintings. Perhaps it is the clarity of what is rendered there that she admires. After all, you were only a toddler when you painted it—three years old, maybe four. And if your placement of subjects is impressionistic—an enormous snail, the sun a blip on the horizon, the trees speckled clusters in the sky hovering above the line-swoop birds—the fact of said subjects, of the sun, the snail, the trees, the birds, is irrefutable.

So what if the snail takes up the entire center of the page, her body a rapacious spiral with a pink, phallic protrusion for a head and a blue fin rising from her back? So what if her body is filled in with that same fleshy pink and blue, but also shaded beige and unmarked white, pockets of the paper clean or smeared with exposed graphite at the nexus of the curling shell?

4.

Your mother didn't keep very much of her own work from art school. There are the two canvas abstract paintings, both of which you've inherited and carried with you from San Diego to Los Angeles to Idaho, one of which hangs in your office and now serves as your Zoom background for classes and meetings. There is a small 8½-by-11 sketch of a pretty woman in profile, her face and hair and shadows smudged in reddish-brown charcoal. The woman's nose is much smaller and rounder than yours, but her hair pulled back in a loose, low bun echoes the almost unvarying style in which you wear your own. Then there is the still life of bottles and jars, the drawing your mother once swore she'd never give you, that now lives in your kitchen beside a thrifted oil painting of wildflowers and citrus fruit. She tells you she likes its placement there—the still life, in your kitchen. She says it doesn't match the rest of the aesthetic in her apartment, where she has gone bold with color: Rothko prints, yellow curtains, an Art Deco–inspired tapestry, red-leather club chairs. Your snail painting and its pair, a pink and yellow abstract bursting with neon, each framed and hanging above the couch.

5.

One morning, she calls you up and asks if you "would like to have her nude."

It is not, as the nickname may suggest, a nude portrait of your mother. It is *Nancy's Nude*, a title her own artist mother bequeathed upon the drawing. The nude, your mother insists, is unattractive. But technically it is one of the pieces, like the still life, of which she is most proud.

You struggle to place the image at first. Unlike the still life, the nude never hung in your family's house. This, perhaps, because it is a very large drawing, at least five feet across in length, and fragile, on browning sketch paper. The charcoal is violent and loud, the lines and shading deep across and around the ripples and curves of flesh-drape topography that is the body of this unknown woman.

Before you recollect these details, however, you agree. Yes, you want the nude, you say. You will hang it in your room, or above the television. There is something in the manner of your mother's asking that suggests inheritance; trust; a shiver of mortality, of speeding time. Then you go to her apartment to look at the nude and recoil when she unrolls the cracking paper. Not because it is an unattractive drawing or an unattractive subject, but because the lines appear, to you, so very angry.

6.

As for you, how often do you mis-see your own intent until you look much closer?

It is not the phallic pink that is the head of the snail. The head is subtle: a small, winking slash of thick and heavy red in the bottom righthand corner of the frame. It has two antennae and a smile. A parallel slash of black inside the body.

What is it, that black? A soul?

7.

When you were twenty-seven, you wrote an essay about your mother's rape. After she told you the story, you wrote breathlessly, finished the draft in a matter of days. Then you asked her to read the essay before it was published—it was your first acceptance, at a reputable and widely read online journal—and your mother, to your relief, gave her blessing.

"Except that isn't how it happened," she'd said. "I mean, the writing is very good. But it isn't true."

It has been ten years since your mother first told you the story, since you first attempted to write about it. The man, the bus stop, the laundry, the knife. Now your mother is seventy, and you are thirty-seven. In these past ten years, you've asked (or let her tell you—depending on the mood, the context) more about the circumstances surrounding that day. You remember and ask more about Gloria Allred, confirm that it was in fact her, at the very start of her career, who sought your mother out as one of many such women to testify against her assailant.

Your mother never tells you what it was that you had gotten wrong in your first essay. Only that it wasn't how it happened to her—or, rather, perhaps, the truth of it for her, how it had felt.

Of course, you think. *How could it ever be?*

8.

Two summers after driving your mother to and from Spokane for the ECT treatments, you once again find yourself ferrying her to hospitals across the Palouse. Your mother needs a colonoscopy. Your mother needs cataract surgery—first one eye, then the other. Your mother has a back spasm and needs to go to urgent care for what she hopes will be a Vicodin prescription. Her body, perpetually moving in and out of intake rooms and recovery rooms. Your body, masked and waiting.

When she visits urgent care, she tries to joke about the Vicodin—"you know, the fun stuff"—and is met with steeled worry in the eyes of the doctor. In the end, though, the doctor concedes, writes the scrip. All the way to the Walmart pharmacy, your mother complains about them making "such a big deal" about the drugs. You bite your tongue and drive.

9.

It would be easier to challenge your mother's hunger for the quick fix of the Vicodin if you didn't harbor your own bad habits. Like your mother before you, you've come to anticipate the tension-melting, solitude-sweetening solace of a drink earlier and earlier, your longstanding five o'clock rule creeping upward into afternoon as the long summer yawns. That you recognize this creeping, this echo, seems to guarantee that someday you will likewise face a reckoning. The thought, a quiet hum against the back of your brain, someplace deep below the gums. Then you swallow and can't hear it anymore.

10.

Next, your mother swallows a camera. The doctors think she may have Crohn's disease, that the intermittent blockages and inflammation, constipation and its opposite, may have a name. To make sure, they bring her to the hospital and give her a large pill with surveillance inside. They say she needs to do this to move forward with possible infusion therapies for Crohn's. They tell her the risk to her health in doing so is minimal. The camera, they say, should pass easily enough within a few days.

But the camera doesn't budge. The camera gets stuck.

This sticking, if it stays, will lead to surgical removal. More than anything, your mother fears another surgery. You fear it too: the waiting, the recovery, the touch and go.

11.

In early summer, you go on two dates with a painter you meet on Hinge. He is nice-looking and seems interesting—his art, his music—but you are not particularly attracted to him until that first date where, over the course of sharing a pizza and salad, you find yourself increasingly desirous of his desire for you: his blatant admiration. In exchange, you ask about his work. He tells you he is making an encaustic piece—burnt wax and oils, a sort of melding of two- and three-dimensional media. Back and forth, you share stories of your families, your education, your travels.

The painter doesn't drink. He tells you he quit because his parents were both problem drinkers and he'd realized by his twenties that he would be, too, if he kept it up. You admire this. You find yourself telling him more than you might have otherwise—about your mother, about your own proclivities. You soften the latter by saying that you've lately realized you can't keep it up, that you have been cutting back. Only half of this is true.

Still, you play the part. You do not order wine. You marvel, as the meal unspools over the course of one hour, then two hours, then three hours, at your comfort without it. You assume this must mean that the painter is special; that there is something real, some authentic openness, possible between you.

After dinner, you and the painter walk beneath the blooming lilacs, and he tells you that you are stunning. He kisses you and you feel the desire to kiss him back—not out of politeness but out of wanting. With thirst. The two of you make out on a bench in a downtown parking lot, feeling one another up like teenagers out past curfew in the dimness of the clouded dark and hissing streetlamps. Finally, he drives away, and you drive home, a little dizzy. He messages you when he gets home safe and uses that word again: *stunning*.

12.

The next day, mining for details, you look up the history of encaustic painting. Then, because you are you, and because you are now smitten with the painter and want to be fluent in his lexicon, you begin to explore complete glossaries of visual and fine arts terminology.

Though you stopped drawing and painting with any regularity as soon as you were old enough for more structured extracurriculars like ballet and soccer, something about being near artists has long felt elemental to your happiness, to your dimensionality as a person. Your college roommate was a fine arts major. You would often set yourself up with your laptop in the common room so you could work on literary analysis papers while she stood nearby, her latest painting-in-progress propped up against the kitchen wall.

Visual art imbues your sense of atmosphere, of home. Your mother's drawings and paintings, hanging in the house before you were conscious. Her own materials, offered to you as toys once you'd learned to use your thumbs. She afforded you the privilege of playing with her charcoals, pastels, oil paints, long before you were old enough to appreciate their quality. You flipped through her art books—Monet, Cassatt, Sargent, Rodin, Chagall—like any other picture books around the house. Later, you would come to value this frame of reference when you traveled with your parents to the DeYoung Museum in San Francisco, the Tate in London, the d'Orsay in Paris.

Now, skimming these museums' websites, their resource pages, you jot down the words that captivate you: *maquette*, *impasto*, *earthwork*, *convergence*, *pentimento*.

13.

The second date with the painter is nowhere near as good as the first. You can feel it almost immediately: something is different. Neither of you is at ease. The painter has invited you over to his house and insists on offering you a glass of wine. It is the cheapest white wine at Target, which he readily admits, and while you cannot blame him (all but several ounces will go to waste), you also taste the diminution of the gesture on your tongue.

The wine flushes straight to your cheeks when he touches your arm. You feel the flush assaulting your face, the heat pricking your skin, exploding across your cheekbones like hives, and excuse yourself to the bathroom where you run cool water over your wrists and smear cosmetic powder across your nose. Afterward, you try to laugh it off. He kisses you, tells you you're beautiful. Still, you can feel the heat, the shame of your body betraying your insecurity in this: a strange man's house, arms, couch. The mismatched manner of your bodies: his, barefoot and in shorts, drinking a smoothie; yours, overdressed in a black silk button-down blouse, your reddened fingers clutching the plastic wineglass with faux sophistication. You wish you had declined the wine. Or, better yet, you wish the wine would transform into a shot of tequila, something sharp and strong and instant in its melting.

14.

After dinner and a walk near the river, you spend the night with the painter. You have sex because he has said he wants to let this evolve and you have said it, too, and sex seems, to you, the logical next step in moving things along.

Before you've even left his house in the morning, he grows distant; says he's still processing his recent breakup, that he's just so busy and so tired. Within days, he texts you to say he can't commit to anything consistent after all.

In response, you try to be sympathetic to his circumstances. You tell him that you understand, but in truth you do not understand. For weeks, you keep trying to maintain some kind of a connection—texting, liking his Instagram posts. He responds just often enough to bait the habit.

Mostly, you wonder how the tables turned on you so very, very fast. How he'd managed to seize you utterly; how you'd managed, in turn, to utterly lose him.

15.

The National Gallery in London defines *pentimento* as "derived from the Italian 'pentirsi,' which means to repent or change your mind."

In visual art, "pentimento is a change made by the artist during the process of painting. These changes are usually hidden beneath a subsequent paint layer. In some instances, they become visible because the paint layer above has become transparent with time."

Famous pentimenti have frequently covered up a scandal, or belied the true complexity of a narrative, a body, a face. John Singer Sargent's *Madame X*, for instance, fixes the once slipped strap on Madame Pierre Gautreau's alabaster shoulder. Her sexuality, the suggestion of nudity, concealed.

Did Sargent, indeed, repent? Did he worry about Gautreau's reputation? Or his own?

16.

In the hope of better understanding your mother, her story, her life, all of the versions of the stories she has told you, all of the versions you can't help but edit in your memory, you ask if you can record a conversation with her, a conversation about her twenty-seventh year. She agrees, provided she can have a drink first.

You ask questions here and there, but mostly let her talk uninterrupted—except for when Lou, with a sly paw, bats at your mother's wispy white hair from her perch on the windowsill, or meows abruptly, interrupting, wanting to be fed. Your mother doesn't talk about the rape itself in this recording so much as the before and after: the apartment she had loved, that the two of you manage to locate on Google Maps, that is truly wonderful with its bougainvillea garden and Spanish tile. She talks about the boyfriend that she'd broken up with just before the assault, the man she ran to afterward despite herself because she didn't want to be alone, didn't want to spend the night in her apartment where the assault had taken place. She talks about her neighbor, a television writer, who later interviewed her about the rape and paid her a one-time fee for her story, then used it as the basis for an episode of the *Mary Tyler Moore* spinoff show, *Lou Grant*. (The Lou in question here is no relation to the cat.)

17.

That night, you search for the episode. Your mother doesn't recall the title, so you look for episodes written and produced by your mother's friend. With their signature one-word titles—"Boomerang," "Venice," "Survival," "Exposé"—episodes of *Lou Grant* are tough to skim. Even reading synopses, you can't find what you are looking for in the seasons from the late 1970s when your mother told you the episode first aired.

Then you see it: "Rape," aired January 12, 1981. The premise, a robbery and rape in the home of a female reporter. The episode is easy to find on YouTube in its entirety. You do not want to, but you need to watch it. You pour a stiff whiskey. Press play. Inadvertently hold your breath when the reporter goes inside her apartment after work, then gathers up laundry and opens a back door to the apartment courtyard.

What happens next, aside from the setting and the physical descriptions of the actors in the scene, lacks only the trappings of your mother's exact life—her dog Kahlua, her Spanish-style apartment—to precisely match the story as she told it to you, as you recorded it, ten years ago. Never, in all your unbidden imaginings, has the story felt so real as it did that night: unspooled in grainy pseudo-fiction on your laptop screen.

18.

When you tell your mother you found the TV episode, she frowns into the phone.

"No, that can't be it," she says.

She explains that the episode she'd been paid for definitely aired before 1981, and that the story wasn't about a female reporter. You do not argue, do not want to tell your mother anything more about the episode you watched, the episode called "Rape." But later she finds it on her own and corroborates what you've already begun to suspect: that her writer friend must have used the story not once, but twice—the second time without permission or payment. That the second iteration was far closer, in its details, to the truth.

19.

Your mother lost her virginity at seventeen to a handsome Italian bus driver named Giorgio. It is the most romantic story she has ever told you: the high school trip to Italy, the way he singled her out among the crowd, their escape, one afternoon, into a sun-warmed field. They even exchanged letters for a time afterward. Very little secrecy or guilt. Very little to regret.

You cannot know for certain. But if you take stock of all your mother's stories about her romantic partnerships and sexual history—all of it, the parts you wanted to hear and all the parts that you did not, the parts she had no one else to tell—Giorgio was possibly not only the first, but also the best.

That promise: that sex and romance could be real and could be hers, together, could even be magical and cinematic like a painting or a film. You wonder if he colored the lenses of everything thereafter—expectations, disappointments. How much more devastating, after such a golden start, the rape must have been. The unmaking of that magic into violence. The dissolution of specialness, a quality she tells you she had felt in her mid-twenties, for a time, in the face of such an assault. That dullness that crept in thereafter, a dullness that became repression during her marriage to your father and has lately curdled into an antisexual stance in nearly all things—relationships, bodies, politics, art.

As for you, sex has always come with risk. Actual danger, or the sense of it. A transaction: of power strategy, negotiation, performance, self-betrayal. Even when you try to give yourself over, let your hunger show, there's always fear beneath your skin. There is always the compulsion to maintain control—of your body, of desire.

Over and over, you pull the slipping strap back up across your shoulder.

20.

Madame X was a social climber, at once seductive and subtle in her lures, a sitter whose reputation demanded the pentimento—the edit to her diamanté strap. She is your favorite Sargent woman: her bold posture, her black dress. Your mother's favorite, meanwhile, is *La Carmencita*. She was a music hall dancer: a performer by trade, haughty in the face of her social restrictions, a challenging sitter, according to Sargent, but likewise a "bewildering superb creature." When she sat for Sargent, her gaze, if hooded, was direct.

Looking at the paintings now, side by side, you see something new: how similar these women are, in some ways, to yourself and to your mother—or at least to versions of yourselves, projections, iterations. *Madame X*, all regal neck and alabaster arms and auburn hair and nasal prominence. A would-be femme fatale, at once exhibiting sophistication and threatening it with her brazen, blinding skin. All the while, looking away from the painter—off into the distance, out of the frame.

As for *La Carmencita*? Her boldness is direct. It is all about the eyes, the gaze, the gaudy insistence of her gold and spangle-laden costume. Her sneering smile, her upturned lip, her hands on her hips.

21.

You find an original Louise Bourgeois exhibition print from Moderna Museet, the Modern Art Museum in Stockholm, on Etsy. The image: *Blue Is the Color of Your Eyes*. It is a painting, more or less, of breasts—five in total, undulating like hills or waves. One blue pair hangs downward against a backdrop of pastel pink. A trio of smaller breasts reaches to meet them, fill the gaps between, from the bottom of the frame.

As with the images that have inspired your tattoos, you admire the frankness, the bodily openness of this painting. Bolder than you are, than you usually feel inside your body. You order the print, put it into a cheap frame, and hang it your dining room. As with the images that have inspired your tattoos, your mother recoils.

"I keep wanting to drape something over it when you're not home," she says.

"In that case, it's a good thing you don't live here," you say back, with a laugh.

She shakes her head, then looks up. From heavily lined yet still exceedingly sharp blue eyes, her grinning glance meets your own.

22.

So often, art does the work of covering over a story as it is. You, as an artist, as a maker of narrative, understand this all too well. And yet without each work of art, we would have neither the hint at truth nor the slant retelling.

You recognize that it wasn't so much a matter of getting the writing of your mother's story wrong that first time you attempted it, all those years ago. It was the fact that such a story is, must be, multitudinous. That there is no single version. That details come and go—some by choice, others by machination of time. That you could change your story to match your mother's story over and over and over and never get it right, not even if you hunted down the criminal records and court proceedings. That your mother may change her way of telling, change her mind about what to share and what to conceal, for the rest of her life.

The changes, the corrections, the edits, the secrets. They imbue one another. They overlap. If you listen closely, perhaps you will at least begin to comprehend a fuller, more complex picture. Of your mother. Of history. Of yourself.

23.

At first, you find it difficult to disassociate the word *repent* from religious contexts—the product, no doubt, of all that Catholic school when you were young. The fact that *pentimento* comes with the far simpler, wholly secular connotation—to change one's mind—is what surprises you.

But as you explore various definitions of the word, you discover more surprises. Besides the expected verb forms—"to regret," "to renounce"—there is also the adjective form that relates to botany: creeping or crawling, like a vine or stem, low to the ground or just below the surface of the earth.

24.

Eventually, your mother passes the camera. No surgery required. Together, you celebrate with drinks and tortilla chips on the patio at the Mexican restaurant downtown.

Then the doctor calls to say that the images from the camera were "inconclusive." No new information. No new treatment for Crohn's. Just more of this uncertainty: if and when your mother will suffer another obstruction and end up in the ER. If and when emergency surgery will be necessary to keep her alive.

25.

That night you'd spent with the painter, all the magic and the chemistry of that first date's lilac-tinted dusk was gone.

There was a mirror on the door, facing the bed. You leaned over, turned your head away from him and to the right. You watched his body arched over your body, his hands gripping your hips. You watched your own body curving up against him, your hair tumbling across your shoulders. In the mirror, your body looked smooth, alternatively curved and narrow in all the right places.

It wasn't that you wanted it to be this way—this depersonalized experience of sex, your faces turned away from one another. It was that you could tell he needed it to be this way and, in that moment, you desperately wanted to be the person—body—to meet his needs. You wanted to watch him experiencing pleasure in your body, presence, givingness. Wanted him, afterward, to love you for it.

When he didn't, you replayed the mental tape from that night over and over in your head. You didn't want to admit that the sex had been bad; that even when he came, and you most certainly did not, the collective atmosphere was one less of satisfaction than relief.

26.

In an 2021 essay for *The Atlantic* titled "The Problem with Being Cool about Sex," Helen Lewis explores several recent books that trouble the notion of twenty-first-century sexual liberation for women, femmes, and female-identifying people still struggling to comprehend the tricky intersection of desire, consent, abandon, and fear. Lewis notes the hyper-prevalence of pornography in the sex lives of millennial and Gen Z individuals and the ways in which a porn-saturated consciousness can't help but focus on the performative aspects of sex. Simply looking at one's partner, it seems, is too much sometimes—too intimate a refusal of the imaginary audience.

Lewis goes on to discuss Amia Srinivasan, author of *The Right to Sex: Feminism in the Twenty-First Century*, who observes that in our post–#MeToo world of supposedly modern sexual mores and consent-driven enlightenment, in a cultural moment where women are superficially encouraged to know what they want and say yes or no with conviction, we still lack an adequate vocabulary to define the many varieties of bad sex that fall short of criminal standards for rape or sexual assault.

Bad sex, in this postulation, might encompass anything from the unwanted to the unsuccessful to the unsatisfying. It might be a mood or a feeling more than an act. It might include countless instances of ambivalent consent, the nebulous *I didn't not want to* or *I wanted something but not that* or *I wanted that but not tonight* kind of sex that constitutes, for many—especially women and femmes—the bulk of sexual experience.

For men, meanwhile, sex poses a direct threat to social constructs of masculinity by asking them to expose themselves emotionally as well as physically. The resultant fear, Lewis contends, is unsurprising—as is the tendency for men to avoid dealing with that fear, in part, by turning to pornography as a sexual playbook and thereby escaping the demand for emotional vulnerability.

It is clear, by the end of the essay, that "being cool about sex" only gets us—as women, as a society—so far.

27.

Your nurse, T, is eight months pregnant. She apologizes for the delay, then asks you to step on the scale. You hang your computer bag ("purse," she says, which it is not) on the proffered hook. It is 4 p.m. and the first pseudo-period day of your cycle—as in, the heavy-gutted, heavy-breasted, bloat-and-cramp before the blood comes day. You are grateful for the lack of blood because it means you can keep this appointment. But you resent the scale: three extra pounds, just to spite your body, as if this appointment, the reason you are here with T and the doctor who is running late isn't bad enough already.

You are here for a colposcopy. Your second, though the first was nearly fifteen years ago, long-enough ago so that you can't remember all the details of the procedure. You look them up before the appointment. A colposcopy allows a gynecologist to investigate abnormal cells inside the cervix. You are here because, once again, your cervix harbors such cells.

The first time, your body nurtured these cells with mutinous abandon. Frozen off, they came back. Lasered off, the threat remained. You didn't feel free of danger until several years' worth of negative HPV tests in a row. Now it has been three years since your last clear pap. This is standard medical procedure. It also means there is no way to place blame. There have been enough men, enough times when you forwent the condoms in the past three years—because it felt better, because he couldn't stay hard, because you thought you might be falling in love—that almost any one of them could be the man who reinfected you. Maybe all of them did. HPV is tricky like that.

All of those men seem lightyears away now. It has been a hungry season. All summer, ever since the painter, you've been sex-starved, gaping and eager. Now it is August. Sitting in the doctor's office, you feel the opposite sensation: a closing in, a metaphorical reaction to the impending acid and iodine and scraping and cutting that can, as the doctor warned, lead to scar tissue; a closing of the cervix. The procedure is not comfortable, by any means. The acid burns, the cone biopsy clicks and cramps. But still, you do not bleed.

You leave, skipping the bulky maxi-pad T leaves out on the counter. You go first to the coffee shop and sit outside, drink a beer. Then you walk all the way home, make supper, edit a manuscript, play with the cat, scoop the curled and gnarled body of a dead wasp from the windowsill with a paper towel. All of this and still: no cramping, no bleeding. Just this winnowing of trust, and of desire.

You do not tell your mother. Out of worry. Out of uncertainty. Out of shame.

28.

After nearly one and a half years of remote teaching, your state university campus reopens for in-person classes in the fall. In the week prior to the start of the semester, you make several practice commutes so you can retrain your body, your habit-creature of a self, to this routine.

It is on one of these pre-semester mornings that you finally get through to the doctor's office for the colposcopy results. You must wait as the receptionist passes you to a nurse on the rotation, and then that nurse goes in search of T.

Finally, T picks up.

Your lesions are mild, she explains. The lowest possible grade. You sit down in a tree-lined breezeway, your body in shadow.

"We'll do another pap in a year," T says. You say thank you. Breathe a sigh of relief.

Then again, now you are back to waiting. That silence and uncertainty beneath your skin, within the very folds of you. A growth rooted at your core. It could die out, or it could reach and grope.

Repent, you think. A creeping vine. Algae bloomed on a rock.

29.

Fall comes early to northern Idaho. Leaves turn by September. Chill crawls beneath the cobwebbed windows well before the equinox. All summer, Lou spent her nights awake and busy, on the hunt. As the weather turns, she returns to you: to your bed, her small body curled against your calves, your knees.

Then, in the final throes of a second summer warmth, a pair of delicate, translucent, blue-winged creatures move in, one in the kitchen and the other in your office. You don't mind these new tenants, but Lou is obsessed with catching them. She can't, of course. They remain on the ceiling. But she trains her attention with the entirety of her body, all her muscles quivering, the blacks of her golden eyes fully waxed, her tail erect. At night, after four or five hours of sleep, she leaves your bed to hunt the bugs. You can tell because it will be so wholly silent for a while. Then comes the smash of rattling stovetop coils.

Lou, jumping down from atop the refrigerator. Her disappointed, yelping mew.

The season marks itself with a widening range of temperatures:

high sun and sweat in the daytime, precipitously cooling at night. Just as quickly as they appeared, the winged tenants are gone. Now the radiators begin to pop and clank with heat. Lou takes to draping herself across the accordioned cast iron after breakfast and before bedtime. "Radiator Cat" and "Little Miss Melting Cat" enter your maternal lexicon as you stroke her soft, warm fur and sip your coffee in the morning. Your mother worries sometimes, and sometimes so do you: that the heat is too much for Lou's small body, that her eyes look weird, drugged, only half-conscious.

But when the first frost arrives and the neighbors downstairs crank the thermostat, Lou is wise enough to know better. She tests the metal with her paws. The metal burns. She does a little dance, then retreats.

30.

In October, you get Bourgeois's *Femme maison, 1947*, tattooed on your left biceps. You love it. Your tattooer, Karla, loves it. Your mother is appalled.

You've stopped by her apartment after working out at the gym to drop off a borrowed Tupperware container, and the residual heat from your workout prompts you to remove your sweatshirt as the two of you chat on her deck. You forget, in doing so, how your mother might react.

"She has a vagina!" Mom squeals in protest. Her outburst—anatomically inaccurate, no less—makes you laugh.

"So do *you*!" you squeal back. "So do I!" You laugh with your eyes, don't fight the smile cracking at the corners of your lips.

Your mother is not amused. She purses her own lips, averts her eyes, shakes her head. Then she closes her door, leaving you alone on the slats of her rickety front porch.

For the first time in this back-and-forth saga of your tattoos and your mother's disapproval, you can feel, with certainty, the silliness of her objection. It still pains you to upset her; an emotional tic you realize may never fully go away. But the subtlety of your *femme*'s little swoop, her inverted triangle, underneath that slight pooch? You love it. The sex, the pooch, the tiny hand waving from the upper lefthand window. Her saggy knees. Her perfect toes.

Your *femme* is just the body and the house for a head. No floorboards. On this point, you and Karla agree.

"I'm pretty sure the floor is actually the patriarchy," you'd told her, as she adjusted the purple stencil on your arm, the two of you standing together, reflected in the mirror. Karla had nodded, her lips empathetic in their purse.

To suit the placement of the tattoo, the floorboards would have fallen right at the valley of your ligaments and blood vessels and skin where the elbow hinges, facilitating movement, bend. As it is, your *femme*'s outturned feet, her little toes, float free. It's like she's levitating. Like she's willed herself to rise.

31.

Read the internet enough, and you can easily imagine yourself a hardened addict if you drink more than two glasses of wine per day. Wander to other corners of the internet, of course--or read books, watch television, dine out at a restaurant--and you will come to assume the opposite: that this habit is completely normal.

For you, it has always been the case—ever since you started, back in Dublin, before your twenty-first birthday, with a daily drink or two—that someone else nearby was drinking more. That, by comparison, your habits seemed moderate. Whether it was your mother or your father or your partner or your friends, you were cast as the temperate one. It is only recently, in the last few years, that the absolute fiction of your innocence, your temperance, has moved into view.

The pandemic seemed the best excuse imaginable to avert your eyes. At first, you leaned into the collective permission, the early Covid-19 zeitgeist of the privileged work-from-home class: to eat and drink and drink and drink, to bake bread and buy random junk online and color-code your bookshelves and rearrange the furniture. How else, the internet reasoned, was one to survive so much uncertainty, so much unwanted solitude?

As the pandemic stretched across the belly of a full year, then two, as your optimistic efforts with the dating apps soured and you started seeking something, anything, in the virtual arms of men you knew you shouldn't be texting in the first place—men you'd already broken up with, men who were married, men who you'd never even met and likely never would—your own belly rounded and grew soft, a distinctive booze-sugar swell to match the puff and pallor of your cheeks.

You capitulated this body: to the one who left a bruise. To the one who liked S&M play and asked if you'd get off on wearing a collar if he told you to (which you knew you wouldn't, at least not with this man, but you said maybe so he wouldn't stop messaging). To the one who came and went, again and again, and you let him, let his name pinging your home screen serve as a glossing over, a fresh coat of paint. To the married one you've known for decades now, your history of mutual indiscretion a kind of dare: *how much further can we go?* To the photos you took of yourself in lingerie to send to these men, photos of your faceless lips and collarbones. To the way you had to twist your torso further and further to the right to trick the camera into winnowing your waist. To the wine or beer or whiskey that you knew would loosen up your fingers and your spine. To this: a cyclical refusal of the real, night after night. An imagined intimacy. A controlled environment. A willful semiconsciousness.

32.

When the painter, whom you haven't heard from since June, messages you in December asking if you'd like to meet up for coffee, you realize you are unsurprised. Happy, or amused, or wary, or eager—but not surprised. This, you think, is how the story is supposed to go.

You wait half a day to reply. You consider—half lucidly, half vengefully—ignoring him, blocking his Instagram. But that would put too abrupt an end to the narrative, a narrative left hanging for six long months, picked up again at last. Even though you know there are only two possible outcomes, you decide to gamble.

Perhaps, like other men before him, he regrets having let you get away. Perhaps, you think, he's changed his mind.

And as for you? How often do you mis-see your own intent, your own motivation, until you look much closer?

33.

Louise Bourgeois believed in repetition as a tool for making sense of things. So many of her images, motifs—the *femmes*, the spiders, the spirals, the cells—appear again and again, each time telling the viewer, and the artist, something new.

In describing her motivation for creating *The Guilty Girl Is Fragile*, Bourgeois explains to interviewer Simona Vendrame: "There is guilt in not living up to one's highest potential. There is guilt from not being able to make yourself understood. There is guilt in not being a good mother. And there is guilt in not being able to make yourself loved."

34.

Something happens at the turn of the new year. You wake up with a hangover. You wake up and look in the mirror, see the purple-gray troughs and sallow puffiness and reaching crow's feet, reaching like the reddened vessels in your eyes, a reach that worries you, that spreads. You search your eyes: the muted blue, the specks of black.

You wake up and reread the painter's texts from the night before, reaching for meaning that would make them stand out against the texts from all your other men, the men who live inside your phone. You bargain with the universe: for the painter's "Happy New Year," a message that arrived at midnight on the dot, to mean something real and true like love. Even in your blurry state, you know this is ridiculous.

You wake up. Return to the mirror. Hear the hum beneath your gums get loud.

Those first few days of 2022, everything you've held inside your body or denied inside your mind revolts; refuses to stay quiet. Your whole body, spurred perhaps by something deeper still inside, wakes up. That molar hum, mounting to a shriek. The toxic, sour pain in your right shoulder, underneath the blade, that crept in before Christmas, a pain that no amount of yoga or ibuprofen seems to fix. All of it, a reckoning with this—your habits, your heredity. The fact that you are thirty-seven years old, and your hair is getting gray and if you are going to disrupt the reaching, waiting, curling thing inside yourself, the thing that keeps you always tight and held, the time for doing so is now.

When the painter writes to tell you, after weeks of texting and flirting, after several coffee dates and walks, that he has "found someone else," you cry—less for the loss of the painter than for yourself, for your decision to put your heart through a second iteration of this, a narrative conclusion already foregone.

You cry and sit on the floor of your apartment and try to play with Lou, who looks at you, your tearstained face, with an expression of mixed confusion and boredom. Her lack of sympathy, rather than upsetting you, forces a laugh from your throat. Between gulps of half-sobbed air, you talk to her. Wave her little feather toys around. Watch her pupils dilate, huge and black, her body taut with purpose.

The next morning, when you wake, your eyes are puffy and swollen. Your shoulder pain is gone.

35.

You start taking baths with Epsom salts at night. A candle and a can of flavored sparkling water and a novel or a book of poems by your side. You've never been a bath taker, at least not since childhood. But you have also decided not to drink for a while, at least to do your best to log some consecutive alcohol-free days, and the bath seems like a healthy proxy. Indeed, after that first night of heat and steam and salt enveloping your body, of the muscle-melting freedom of your bones and skin and fear unfolded in the tub, the way everything you couldn't speak or feel rose out of you in beads of sweat—dewing the skin of your biceps and forearms and nose, curling the small hairs at your neck—you could not, cannot, get enough.

At first, Lou panics. She watches from the doorway, then from her perch on the toilet seat, intermittently standing up on her hind legs, her little paws gripping urgently at the tub's rim, trying to make sense of this alarming turn of events, of the accumulated water and your naked body and the fuzzy atmosphere.

Then, after half a dozen episodes like this, Lou calms down. Begins to curl up on the bathmat, underneath the squat side table you found to hold your glasses and your books and close her eyes or clean her belly and her toes until you've finished and released the drain.

36.

The snow won't stop. It is a confusing season. You wait for rainstorms, for the water warmth and melt and hints of green.

In the cold, you miss alcohol less than you miss its quick, exacting heat: the way a sip of wine or whiskey swiftly warms that place inside your chest behind your heart. The baths help. Sleeping helps. Vanity—the skin around your eyes, how it bounces back, plumps itself, within mere days—helps, too.

Sometimes, it feels like you are in control: of your drinking, via not drinking, and therefore of your life. Other times, you are wary of this feeling.

Then the storms roll in. One storm, in particular. All afternoon, clouds like bruises, purple-gray and low and heavy in the sky. The way the change in light appears to darken all the leaves on all the trees, turn their branches to obsidian. The air sits soft and still, neither hot nor cold. The air is waiting.

In your body, something rises. You feel an electric pulse of energy moving up and out, reaching along your spine, along your jaw.

Red wine, you think, will let it out. Yes. Red wine and a storm.

For two hours, you pace your apartment and find tasks to busy yourself in attempt to undo this desire. Instead, the desire mounts. It has its teeth in you. At 8 p.m., you get into your car and drive down the hill to the market. The rain is barely spitting in the light wind. You buy a bottle of wine, something Italian. Go home. Open it. Pour a taste. The taste is sweet and warm and lush. You pour a glass. It is a magic trick: the thunder rolls just as you settle on the couch, tilt your head back, let the ruby stuff seize at your throat. The storm unleashes itself upon your window screens. Lou perches on the couch, rapt. You drink and drink. With every sip, the flavor loses something of its richness.

The days that follow unfold like this:

You recognize the electric current in your body as all that molar shrieking and bathtub sweating and water-weighted sky working together to shake you at your core. To change your center of gravity. To loosen the coil, permit it to soften and stretch from the inside out.

You come to know, with solemn clarity, that you won't stand steady in this new gravitational field until you stop drinking—not just for a few days or weeks or even months, but indefinitely. You also know, as suddenly and deeply as you can imagine knowing, that you are ready. That you are terrified, but hungry for this strange and wild change. That your desire for wine the night of the storm had been the opposite of freedom: had been an effort to maintain a controlled environment, familiar and flat. To diminish the energy, when it rose in you like that, first to a manageable tenor, then to a languid thud. To diminish anything, really, in the realm of genuine feeling and knowingness—anger, desire, terror—into something docile, something you could silence or mold into submission, mold into the shape of the emotion you thought you were supposed to want or feel or exhibit.

That the wine itself, for you, where it had once seemed like permission to transgress, was now no longer a release but in fact a refusal of the world.

You don't stop immediately. It takes a few days. You have a sense that you will know when it is time. You go to the market, go to the wine shop, go to the specialty beer bar like you always have, and you buy whatever you are drawn to—a Belgian beer in a tall green bottle with a witchy green woman on the label, an expensive organic red blend that promises smoke and earth against your tongue. You open and sip and stop when you are bored with one and ready to try the other. You try too many different things in a row and feel the familiar headache sprouting at your temples, the familiar swim and swampiness of your thoughts. You drink a little more then, even though none of it tastes good to you, even though you know that you will feel worse for those extra nips and pours come morning.

You do it anyway. With each instance of thinned-out taste, as everything begins to bleed together and the flavors curdle and merge into sameness, you recognize that you are on the verge of being finished. You take this recognition to the edge.

In the morning, you feel sick. Underneath that sickness, somewhere between the tight breath trapped in your chest and the nausea in your belly, there is a little flutter of buoyancy: because you recognize, for the first time since that first sip of Miller High Life from a solo cup at a dorm party during your freshman year of college, that you can and will and do, today, choose to never feel this way again. You choose it today, and you intend to choose it tomorrow. Day by day.

One by one, you pour the contents of every open bottle in your apartment down the drain.

37.

The geese return to fly over town, as they do each year in spring.

Your mother says she'd like to draw Lou someday, maybe even paint a kitty portrait like the one in *Bell, Book, and Candle*, a 1960s mystery movie with Jimmy Stewart and Kim Novak and Novak's real-life cat, Pyewacket, that your mother has watched on TCM at least half a dozen times.

"It's really terrible, the movie," your mother says. "But the cat is amazing."

You Google the portrait of Pyewacket. It, too, is amazing. Abstract blue and orange-red and black angles and orbs bear up the body of the sleek white cat. It is as if he stands at the helm of a psychedelic ship.

Mom rummages around inside your storage drawers and finds your charcoal pencils. Starts a rough sketch of Lou one afternoon over a glass of wine, her model seated just above her shoulder on the couch amid a semi-permanent coating of cat hair. Lou's eyes are half closed, little black-gold slits. You perch your umpteenth can of flavored seltzer water on the armchair and take photo after photo of your mother as she works.

Mom never did give you her nude. It needs a frame, which will likely be expensive, and anyway the having of the drawing doesn't feel so urgent anymore now that Mom is over all the time. With the return to campus at the start of spring semester, the two—that is, three—of you pick up where you left off in the fall. Each day you go to work, your mother visits Lou. It becomes a steady rhythm. Mornings, you get dressed, strap on a face mask, and go to campus to teach. Soon after your car departs, your mother's snappy black and orange Mini Cooper arrives.

She "putters," as she calls it, tidying regardless of whether you've tidied or not. She does your laundry. She watches cooking shows (a favorite: *Jacques and Julia at Home*). She plays with Lou, her "grand-kitty," building worlds of upturned brown bags and tennis balls, old wine corks and feather toys around the living room.

When you get home from work, it looks as though a human toddler lives here. As you unpack your things, you find the evidence of your mother everywhere: how she drapes dishtowels over the clean dish rack instead of hanging them up or puts the reusable cat-food lids into your fruit bowl instead of into a drawer. At first, this annoyed you. As time passes, the repetition settles in with you, with Lou, with the space the three of you have come to share.

In the ways that really matter, you and your mother aren't so different after all. You both love Lou. You both love, as the weather turns, to listen to the geese.

This is us now, you think, as you fold the towel, hang it on the oven door.

NOTES

A Broom to Remove the Dust

Irving Reti, "Electroconvulsive Therapy Today," http://hopkinsmedicine.org.

Jean Frémon, *Now, Now, Louison*, trans. Cole Swensen (New York: New Directions, 2019).

Stefanie Pettit, "Determination Preserves Home as Development Surrounds It," *Spokesman-Review* (Spokane, WA), June 30, 2011.

Louise Bourgeois, *The Guilty Girl Is Fragile*, in *Louise Bourgeois: The Complete Prints and Books* (New York: Museum of Modern Art, 2001).

"Bernadette Soubirous," in *Wikipedia: The Free Encyclopedia*, https://en.wikipedia.org.

Exhibit label, *Louise Bourgeois: Ode to Forgetting*, Jordan Schnitzer Museum of Art, Washington State University, Pullman, May 21–August 10, 2019.

On Becoming

David S. Moore, *The Developing Genome: An Introduction to Behavioral Epigenetics* (Oxford University Press, 2017).

"The Biology of Sex," *TED Radio Hour*, May 8, 2020, https://www.npr.org.

Interlude: Background Music

"White Zinfandel," in *Wikipedia, The Free Encyclopedia*, https://en.wikipedia.org.

Woman House

Louise Bourgeois, *Louise Bourgeois: Drawings and Observations* (New York: Little, Brown, 1995).

George Cukor, dir., *The Philadelphia Story*, Metro-Goldwyn Mayer, 1940.

Mignon Nixon, *Fantastic Reality: Louise Bourgeois and a Story of Modern Art* (Cambridge, MA: MIT Press, 2005).

Double Exposure

Joanne Kyger, *The Tapestry and the Web* (San Francisco: Four Seasons Foundation/City Lights Books, 1965).

Joanne Kyger, *Strange Big Moon: The Japan and India Journals: 1960–1964* (Berkeley, CA: North Atlantic Books, 2000).

Joanne Kyger, Letters to Philip Whalen, 1958–1965, Reed College Library, Special Collections and Archives.

Maggie Nelson, *On Freedom: Four Songs of Care and Constraint* (Minneapolis: Graywolf, 2021).

Distance Instructions

Jia Tolentino, *Trick Mirror: Reflections on Self-Delusion* (New York: Random House, 2019).

A Kind of Chrysalis

Louise Bourgeois, "Self-Expression is Sacred and Fatal: Statements," in *Louise Bourgeois: Designing For Free Fall, by* Christiane Meyer-Thoss (Zurich: Ammann Verlag, 1992), 179.

John J. O'Connor, "An England Where Heart and Purse Are Romantically United," *New York Times*, January 13, 1996.

"*Sanditon*'s Rose Williams on Starring in the New Austen Adaptation—Feminism, Racism, and Nooky," *The Times (London)*, August 23, 2019.

“Class” (noun), *Oxford English Dictionary*, 2010, https://www.oed.com. Reproduced with permission of the licensor through PLSclear.

Louise Bourgeois, loose sheet of writing (excerpt), September 16, 1957, LB-0140. Courtesy of Louise Bourgeois Archive / Easton Foundation, New York.

Pentimento

“Pentimento,” glossary (paintings), National Gallery, London, https://www.nationalgallery.org.uk.

Neha Pophale, “Discovering a Pentimento: A Secret under Paintings,” *Art Fervour*, October 3, 2020, https://www.artfervour.com.

“*La Carmencita* by John Singer Sargent,” Metropolitan Museum of Art, New York, https://www.metmuseum.org.

Helen Lewis, “The Problem with Being Cool about Sex.” *The Atlantic*, September 3, 2021.

Amia Srinivasan, *The Right to Sex: Feminism in the Twenty-First Century* (New York: Farrar, Straus, and Giroux, 2021).

Louise Bourgeois, “*The Guilty Girl Is Fragile*,” in *Louise Bourgeois: The Complete Prints and Books* (New York: Museum of Modern Art, 2001).

ACKNOWLEDGMENTS

In some ways, I believe this book—even though it is not my first—has always been the thing I most needed to write, the book that brought me to writing. My first attempts at essay and memoir swirled around my mother's stories and the intersections of our lives, and while most of those drafts fell by the wayside once I decided to pursue an MFA, something about the solitude and silence of the pandemic, years later, forced them back to the surface. Harrowing though it was, I'm grateful for that time: it afforded me the space to consider and confront many questions that have been nagging at me for most of my adult life, and to discuss them with my mother in a rare, uninterrupted pocket of presence and attention that was, and continues to be, deeply meaningful—to my writing, thinking, and living.

Thank you to my mother for taking that time with me. For understanding the art and craft that go hand in hand with writing down ideas and feelings into something that extends beyond the personal, the diaristic, and for granting me permission to interview her, record our conversations, and explore the details of her past and our shared present.

I would like to express my gratitude to the many readers and colleagues who have supported me and my writing—of this book itself, and of the fragments and drafts that got me here. Thank you to Margaret Wappler and Chris Daley, to Jessica Ripka, Kim Young, Andrea Ciannavei, Teri Carson, Louisa Levine, Camille Lowry, and everyone else from those magical evenings with Writing Workshops Los Angeles. Thank you to early readers Tonya Canada, Sarah Ciston, Chris Gaumer, Dierdre Sugiuchi, Mary-Kim Arnold, and others from the Tin House summer workshop community. My sincere thanks and gratitude to my MFA cohort at the University of Idaho, with special appreciation for my creative nonfiction peers, especially Sarah VanGundy and Courtney Kersten, and for my mentors Kim Barnes and Brian Blanchfield. Thanks to my colleagues and friends at Washington State University, with particular gratitude to Colin Criss and Grant Maierhofer, for artistic companionship and good humor. A heartfelt thanks to Anne Horowitz for being an astute reader and brilliant editor, not to mention an invaluable guide to the publishing world. And thank you to the many other writers and teachers who have influenced my thinking and sense making within these pages, directly or indirectly, including Maggie Nelson, Brett Millier, Melissa Febos, Aisha Sabatini Sloan, Arianne Zwartjes, Jia Tolentino, Amia Srinivasan, Katherine Angel, Mignon Nixon, Lauren Elkin, Annie Ernaux, Kate Zambreno, Rebecca Solnit, Leslie Jamison, and—of course—Joanne Kyger and Louise Bourgeois.

Thanks to the organizations that have provided time and funding to support this project, including the Idaho Commission for the Arts and the National Endowment for the Arts, and the Kimmel Harding Nelson Center for the Arts. Many thanks as well to the journals where versions of essays from this collection first appeared, including "A Broom to Remove the Dust" in *Seneca Review* (July 2021), "Twenty-Seven" in *The Rumpus* (May 2013), "Milk Clock" in *New Delta Review* (December 2018), and “Still Life” in *Revolution House* (December 2013).

Thank you to both my parents for supporting my (sometimes uncomfortable) aspirations as a writer of nonfiction and memoir. Your open-mindedness and generosity mean the world to me.

Finally, to Alijah: thank you for being my partner and my biggest support throughout the journey of finding a home for this book. *Woman House* may be a mother-daughter love story, at its core—but writing it, making the choices engendered by the process of crafting these pages, carved out space in my life for our love story. Thank you for finding me, and for your patience, tenderness, ready laughter, and curious spirit. Lou and I are so lucky to have you.

JUNIPER PRIZE FOR CREATIVE NONFICTION

This volume is the sixth recipient
of the Juniper Prize for Creative Nonfiction,
established in 2004 by the
University of Massachusetts Press
in collaboration with the
UMass Amherst MFA Program
for Poets and Writers, to be
presented annually for an outstanding
work of creative nonfiction.
Like its sister award, the
Juniper Prize for Poetry established
in 1976, the prize is named in honor
of Robert Francis (1901–1987),
who lived for many years at
Fort Juniper, Amherst, Massachusetts.

www.ingramcontent.com/pod-product-compliance
Lightning Source LLC
LaVergne TN
LVHW091136080826
845145LV00008B/2170